Notably I

Recipes   Fes

Vesterheim, The Norwegian-American Museum, Decorah, Iowa.

by Louise Roalson
Graphic Design: Esther Feske
Photography: Joan Liffring-Zug
  unless otherwise indicated
Recipe Editors: Miriam Canter and   .
  Norma Wangsness
Researchers and Contributing Writers:
  Kay Eginton, Julie Jensen McDonald,
  Jane Viemeister and John Zug

Dedication

This little book is dedicated to all those who have helped to develop Vesterheim into one of the finest ethnic museums in America where the descendants of Norwegian immigrants such as Eric, Brad and Craig Roalson can find the preservation and interpretation of their heritage.

Contents

Christmas at the Skaugstads (cover)

Marilyn Skaugstad of Iowa City, Iowa, posed with her Christmas baking for the cover photo. "Who would have thought as I sat with my elbows propped on Grandma Olson's big kitchen table, watching her bake, that forty years later I would be recalling her Norwegian heritage and customs and foods to be published in a book about Norwegian-Americans? With flour and dough flying, she told me about her summers as a little girl spent high in the mountains above the Sørfjorden Fjord making flatbread on an old wood-fired cookstove in a little cabin while she tended the sheep for her family.

"With her 'letter' in hand, she came to America in the early 1900s and worked for a family in Wisconsin. Eventually she married my grandfather, Ole J. Olson, whose family also came from Norway. They farmed a beautiful big farm in Humboldt County, Iowa.

"My father, L.E. Mosbach, of Irish-German descent, used to tease my mother, Esther, saying that Norwegian girls made the best wives, *one* of the reasons being that they were wonderful cooks. She certainly is, and she has helped my sister and me continue the customs of Norwegian baking and cooking. We have all visited Grandma Olson's farm in Ullensvang, Norway, where our relatives still live.

"When I married my husband, Charles, I certainly reinforced my Norwegian heritage. His father came from Land, Norway, to Bode, Iowa, where he met and married Albie Tufte, whose family came from Telemark. Bode, a very Norwegian community, still has annual smorgasbord suppers. My four sisters-in-law and I enjoy sharing recipes and customs from Norway. Christmas is always fun and full of good food from Norwegian family recipes—*lutefisk, lefse,* Norwegian meatballs..."

Inside Front Cover:

A display at Vesterheim, the Norwegian-American Museum, Decorah, Iowa, represents a traditional Christmas Eve meal of decorated butter, flatbread on a wood-turned pedestal and fish pudding molded in the form of a fish. A devotional book contains daily scriptural readings, basic to the family library.

Special Acknowledgment

The author, editors and publisher give a special thank you to Dr. Marion Nelson, director of the Norwegian-American Museum at Decorah, Iowa, and his wife Lila Nelson, who gave unselfishly of their time and knowledge. Without their help, this book would not have been possible.

Acknowledgments

In addition to the many contributors who are mentioned with their essay or recipe, we would like to thank Charles Roberts, editor, and David Archie, publisher, of *The Iowan* magazine, Des Moines; Don Padilla and David Hakensen of Padilla and Speer, Inc. of Minneapolis; The Rev. R. A. Olsen, retired pastor of the Chapel in the Hills, Rapid City, S.D.; the Rapid City Convention-Visitors Bureau; Jack Anundsen of Decorah, Iowa; Mary Lou Sollien and the Nordic Fest committee, Decorah; Sigurd Daasvand, former editor, *Nordisk Tidende,* Brooklyn, N.Y.; Prof. Einar Haugen, Belmont, Mass.; Del Bjerkness, director of Language Villages, Concordia College, Moorhead, Minn.; Mrs. Marcy Winner, Little Norway, Blue Mounds, Wis.; Jim Roalson, Custer, S.D.; Jean Newkirk and Prof. Harry Oster, Iowa City; Darrell Henning, curator, and Bill Musser, staff member, Vesterheim, the Norwegian-American Museum, Decorah; Morton and Connie Strand and Mrs. John R. Christianson, Decorah; Henning C. Boe, editor, *Western Viking,* Seattle, Wash.; Marianne Forssblad, Nordic Heritage Museum, Seattle, Wash.; Prof. Virginia Myers, The University of Iowa, Iowa City; Fran and Gustave von Groschwitz, New York City; the Norwegian Information Service in the United States, Inger Lavik Opdahl, deputy director, New York; Trade Commission of Norway, New York; Larry Waller, executive vice-president Cedar Rapids-Marion Chamber of Commerce; Margie Fletcher, Ann Urness Gesme and Toini Saxegaard Landis, Cedar Rapids, Iowa; and the Royal Norwegian Ministry of Foreign Affairs, Oslo, Norway.

Library of Congress Catalog Card Number: 82-81569
ISBN 0-941016-05-6

Copyright 1982 Penfield Press
Published by Penfield Press
215 Brown Street
Iowa City, Iowa 52240 U.S.A.

Printed by Julin Printing Co., Monticello, Iowa

H.M. King Olav V of Norway (center), honorary chairman of Vesterheim, the Norwegian-American Museum, met with board members at the 1975 dedication of the museum. King Olav came to America for the sesquicentennial celebration of Norwegian immigration. At right is Marion Nelson, director of Vesterheim. *Photograph by Darrell Henning, Vesterheim curator.*

It All Began in 1825

The year 1975 was celebrated by Norwegian-Americans as the sesquicentennial (150 years) of the start of Norwegian emigration to the New World.

What happened in 1825? That was the year that the sloop *Restoration* sailed the Atlantic, bringing into New York harbor 52 Norwegians plus a baby born to the captain and his wife five weeks before the landing.

It was a long (July 4 to October 9) and perilous voyage undertaken by people who were aware of the dangers and who willingly risked their lives to reach the New World, to become a part of its great challenge and to share its cherished freedoms. Described as "a small, one-masted vessel originally rigged fore-and-aft with a jib, mainsail, and often topsails and staysails," this "Norwegian Mayflower" was less than half the size of the 1620 Mayflower.

The man responsible for this adventure was Cleng Peerson, who spent three years in America and returned to Stavanger in 1824 to tell the people of religious freedom, political equality and economic opportunity in America.

Peerson met the group when the sloop arrived at New York.

The new Americans stayed together, settling in the Kendall area of New York state (near Buffalo), on the shore of Lake Ontario. Here they spent the next ten years. It was from here that Peerson began a long walk of perhaps 2,000 miles in search of a better site in the west.

The area Peerson selected was only 70 miles west and a little south of Chicago—the Fox River Valley with its rich, level and fertile land, today dotted with towns, two of which are named Norway and Stavanger. The migration from New York State to the Ottawa-La Salle County area of Illinois began in 1834.

The 53 who arrived on the *Restoration* (Restauration)—so named because it was repaired and rebuilt for the voyage—became known as the "Sloopers." In 1925, the Slooper Society of America was organized to perpetuate the memory of the Sloopers.

A collection of mementos from the original voyage was given to the Norwegian-American Museum, Decorah, Iowa, where it can be seen today.

Dates in History

12,000 B.C.

People were living in the areas of Norway where the ice mass of the last glacier was receding. Hunting and fishing were the major sources of livelihood. A 4,000-year-old rock carving depicts a human figure on skis.

800-1000 A.D.

For pillaging, trading or settling, Norwegian Vikings sailed to England, Scotland, Ireland, Normandy (France), the Isle of Man, the Hebrides, Spain, Sicily and the Near East.

874

Iceland was settled by Norwegians. The Icelandic Althing (parliament), established about 930, is the world's oldest legislative body.

982

Eric the Red discovered Greenland and named this ice-covered land for the stretch of green he found along the southern coast, which the Norwegians settled.

1002

Leif Ericson, thought by some to be the son of Eric the Red, landed on the east coast of North America, calling it 'Vinland' because of grapevines he found growing there in what is today the area of Newfoundland. House foundations and other artifacts discovered on Newfoundland in 1963 are believed to be from Norse settlers who were in America nearly five centuries before Columbus.

1030

Norway was converted to Christianity by King Olaf Haraldsson, also known as Saint Olaf. Special rights of inheritance which protect the oldest son in retention of land also date from this time.

1066

William the Conqueror, seventh generation Viking ruler of Normandy, conquered England, built Windsor Castle, and became the first Norman king of England.

Mid-1300s

Black Plague killed almost half the population of Norway.

1387-1814

Norway was ruled by kings of Denmark.

1814

The Treaty of Kiel penalized Denmark for its support of Napoleon by giving Norway to Sweden. Before the transition was carried out, Norway declared itself independent. The constitution, the parliament and a degree of independence were retained even after Norway became subject to the Swedish crown.

1825

The first Norwegian ship organized for emigration sailed to the United States; the population of Norway at this time was about one million.

1835-1924

At least 750,000 Norwegians immigrated to America. Still, the population more than doubled in Norway as a result of smallpox vaccination, better nutrition made possible by the introduction of the potato from America and other health advances. Today there are over 3½ million Norwegian-Americans. This is only slightly less than the present population of Norway.

1844

Claus L. Clausen became the first pastor to serve a Norwegian congregation in the United States. His first church at Muskego, Wisconsin, stands today, well-preserved, on the campus of Lutheran Theological Seminary, St. Paul, Minn.

1905

Norway declared its complete independence. Charles, brother of King Christian X of Denmark, became King Haakon VII of Norway.

1909

Oslo and Bergen were connected by a spectacular railway.

1914

World War I began; Norway remained neutral, but many of its ships were sunk by submarines.

1917

Norwegian Lutheran Church in America was formed as a union of three synods— Norwegian and Hans Nielsen Hauge's, both dating from the 1840s, and the United Norwegian Lutheran Church, which was formed in 1890. The total membership was nearly 1,200,000.

1940-45
Norway was occupied by Nazi Germany. There was active Norwegian resistance.

1946
Norway became a founding member of the United Nations; Trygve Lie of Norway, his country's foreign minister at that time, was elected U.N. secretary general.

1957
King Haakon VII died and was succeeded by his son, King Olav V. King Olav can trace his ancestry back 34 generations to King Harald the Fairhaired who united Norway in 872.

1960
Lutheran Church in America (the word "Norwegian" had been dropped in 1946) merged into the new American Lutheran Church.

1971
Drilling of oil in the North Sea got underway off the coast of Norway near the city of Stavanger.

1975
150th anniversary of the first modern emigration to America; King Olav V came to America for the Sesquicentennial Celebration.

Norway

Once primarily rural with each family self-reliant, Norway today is prosperous and industrialized. Almost 70 percent of the people live in urban areas.

Norway imports 60 percent of its food. In 1950, 27 percent of the working population of Norway was engaged in farming, forestry and fishing; today, only 8 percent. Less than one percent of the nation's work force is engaged in fisheries, but fishing, the oldest industry, is still healthy. Norway ranks sixth in the world in quantity taken from the seas.

More than two-thirds of the catch is exported, but dried, salted, frozen and canned fish products make up less than 10 percent of Norway's exports. Norway exports aluminum, ferro-alloys, nitrate fertilizers, tools, machinery, ships, oil, and electronic and telecommunication products.

Traditionally a seafaring nation, Norway has a merchant fleet of about 850 ships, or 6% of the world's tonnage. Most of Norway's modern vessels carry goods between different foreign ports, never actually docking in Norway.

Norway's coastline is 15,000 miles long. Three-fourths of the people live within 10 miles of salt water. Norway is so mountainous that only 4 percent of its 125,000 square miles is cultivated. Cattle and sheep graze in the mountains.

Along the coasts are 50,000 islands, which help to protect the mainland from storms. Norway has about 1700 glaciers.

The waterfalls are spectacular and have been harnessed for hydro-electric energy. Narrow fjords reach as far as 100 miles inland from the sea. Some are only 500 yards across, yet the mountains on either side are 3,000 feet high. The longest is Sognefjord.

Almost one-fourth of the country is forest land, mostly spruce and pine, but also birch and other deciduous trees.

Winters are long. Norway is snow-covered for four to six months. The weather is fairly mild, however, because of the Gulf Stream which flows north along the coast keeping ports ice free year round.

The period of the Midnight Sun—when the sun never sinks below the horizon—is longer the further north you go. In Tromsø, the largest city in North Norway, this period is May 20-July 23. Hammerfest is the northernmost town in the world.

In area, Norway is the fifth largest European country, but in population density it is the lowest, except for Iceland. The only minority group is the Lapps, who live in the north. Ten percent of the Lapps lead the traditional nomadic life of reindeer herders.

There are two official languages in Norway—standard Norwegian *(bokmål)* and New Norwegian *(nynorsk)*. Nynorsk is based on local dialects.

Norway is a parliamentary democracy. The king is the head of state; executive power is in the cabinet under the prime minister.

5

The Specialties of Norway

Some Norwegian foods are scarcely ever found outside of the nation. One of these is *gravlaks*, uncooked and marinated salmon. In early times it was put into the ground (into its own "grave"). Today a salmon is covered with salt, sugar and dill and put under a weight for several days. It is sliced very thinly and served chilled as an addition to the smorgasbord.

Reindeer meat is a familiar item on the menu in some Norwegian restaurants.

In the days before electric freezers and modern transportation, *spekemat* (cured and dried meats) was a necessity for some remote farm families. Three popular dried meats are *fenalår*, *spekeskinke* and *spekekjøtt*. These meats and other dried food were hung in the storehouse, or *stabbur*. Even today, each farmhouse has its own *stabbur*. *Fenalår* is a leg of lamb that has been soaked in sweetened brine, smoked and then hung in the air to dry. It could be kept for several years. *Spekeskinke* is a ham prepared like *fenalår*. According to legend, *spekeskinke* should be laid away in November and will be ready to eat when the cuckoo returns to Norway and lets out its first call in the spring. Urban housewives now skip the work and buy it ready to serve from the butcher. *Spekekjøtt* is cured dried beef.

Lutefisk (lye fish) is first soaked in water for several days, then in lye made from birch ash or in a mixture of water and caustic soda, then soaked in water. Any *lutefisk* fans today are most likely to buy it at the store, ready for boiling in salted water It can also be purchased in frozen form. *Lutefisk* is usually served with melted butter and accompanied by boiled potatoes.

Gjetost is a caramel-colored cheese made from goat's milk. It is not widely available in America.

Rull is spiced, rolled and pressed mutton or calf. *Sylte* is headcheese made of pork. Both are traditional on the Christmas smorgasbord.

Cloudberries, or *multer*, are yellow berries that grow wild in mountain plateaus. They are scarce, and whoever finds a patch keeps secret the location.

Aquavit (*akevitt*) is a distilled liquor made of potatoes and grain and may be flavored with caraway. The name means "water of life." One Norwegian brand, *Linie*, is so-called because it travels in oak casks aboard cargo ships from Norway to Australia and crosses the "line" (equator). Whether it is the motion of the ship or the change in temperature is not certain, but the long journey is said to improve the flavor.

At the table the bottle is often encased in ice.

Aquavit is colorless and potent. It must not be diluted with ice cubes or a mix, but is served icy cold in a glass so small that it will be emptied in one gulp. It is usually served with a beer chaser and the beer must never be chilled.

Toasting often "opens" the meal. You do not begin eating until the *"skål"!*

Norwegians tend to eat a hearty breakfast which includes a glass of milk. Unlike the Danes, they do not favor sweets for breakfast. People often take a sandwich to work and carry it into a cafeteria where it is perfectly acceptable to order only coffee. The evening meal is early, from 4 to 4:30. Sandwiches or pastry with tea and milk at 9 p.m. is customary.

Water and coffee are not usually served with meals. Instead, beer, pop or sparkling water are offered. Following the meal, coffee and pastry are served in the living room.

Norwegians' favorite herb is dill, the favorite flavoring almond and the spice cardamom.

Norway is the longest country in Europe. Food preferences vary tremendously from north to south and methods of preparing the same food differ from one valley to another because the mountains tended to bar communication.

Wherever you are, in Norway or in a Norwegian-American home, your hostess may say, *"Velkommen til bords"* (welcome to the table) or *"Vær så god"* (be so good) when dinner is ready. After dining, you can tell her *"Tusen takk for maten!"* (a thousand thanks for the food.)

Human Realities Onstage

The Drama of Henrik Ibsen

The towering talent that was Norway's contribution to world drama could have languished in a provincial apothecary shop if Henrik Johan Ibsen had followed his youthful intention.

Born at Skien on March 20, 1828, the shy, introspective lad moved to the coastal town of Grimstad to become a druggist's apprentice. Then he decided to study at the University in Oslo but was sidetracked by the theatrical scene in that city and Bergen.

Ibsen tried his hand at writing some imitative plays, but he soon recognized the dramatic possibilities of his own internal conflicts. The result was works of profound originality that caused shock, surprise and enthusiasm—or condemnation—depending on one's view. He became the strongest creator of realistic, social, contemporary plays in the 19th century.

Ibsen's first masterpiece was *Brand*, written in 1866 and followed the next year by the beloved *Peer Gynt. A Doll's House* made him world famous, and he showed the perverted results of feminine frustration in modern society in *Hedda Gabler.*

Ibsen's final plays were judgments on his own life—unforgettable, poetic expressions of the questioning, disquieting time in which he lived and wrote. Every civilized person has been affected by his life and work—Norway's gift to the world.

—*Julie Jensen McDonald*

Storm and Rainbow

The Art of Edvard Munch

The paintings of Edvard Munch have much in common with the rugged, awesome scenery of his native Norway. They command attention and repay it with a deep thrill.

The artist who was born into a respectable, middle-class family in 1863, said, "We should stop painting interiors with people reading and women knitting. We should paint living people who breathe and feel and suffer and love." He did exactly that.

One of the best-known works from Munch's monumental cycle of paintings, *The Frieze of Life,* is *The Scream,* and this is how he describes its genesis: "One evening I was walking along a path—on one side lay the city and below me the fjord. I was tired and ill. I stopped and looked out across the fjord —the sun was setting—the clouds were dyed red like blood. I felt a scream pass through nature; it seemed to me that I could hear the scream. I painted this picture—painted the clouds as real blood. The colors were screaming."

Munch's early exhibitions met with hostility, but his friend Henrik Ibsen told him, "the more the enemies, the more the friends."

The artist had gained considerable fame by the time of his death in 1944, and the universal significance of his work was fully appreciated by the 1960s. He is often referred to as the Father of Expressionism.

Munch was forced to sell some of his paintings in order to live, but in many cases he made a replica for himself. His prodigious body of work—1,000 paintings, 4,500 drawings and watercolors and 6 sculptures—was willed to the city of Oslo. The Munch Museum at Tøyen, Oslo, was built between 1960 and 1963 to house this remarkable collection.

—*Julie Jensen McDonald*

Music from Norway

Norwegian vocal music before the mid-19th century existed in many forms, including the impressive cattle calls known as *lokk,* a combination of singing, shouting and talking.

The performer, generally a woman, shouts words like *"koma da, bane, a stakkare"* ("come now, children, poor things"), calls the cows by name, sings wide vocal leaps and vocalizes on a high pitch.

In traditional country vocal music a type of poetry was used that consisted of four lines of two nearly identical couplets called *stev.*

The *Hardingfele Violin* (Hardanger fiddle) was played principally in western Norway from Hardanger to Sunnfjord and in the central valleys. It has a wealth of ornamental detail, short neck and fingerboard, and long "f" holes. Four sympathetic strings under the four that are played create a drone effect.

Dances for which the Hardanger fiddle was played were in two overall rhythms. In triple time, the dances were called *springar, springleik, pols* and *runnom.* In double time, they were called *halling, gangar* and *ril.*

Ole Bull

In Europe, the Norwegian Ole Bull (1810-1880) is remembered as one of the great violinists of all time. He was conductor of an orchestra in Oslo and in 1832 he performed with Chopin.

In America, he is remembered for bringing 800 Norwegians in 1852 to Pennsylvania, where he had purchased 11,144 acres of land for a dollar an acre to provide homes for them. The sale proved to be fraudulent, and the settlers were forced to move on.

Bull's first concert in the United States was in 1843. There is an Ole Bull State Park in Pennsylvania near "Oleana," as the land site was known. There is a monumental statue of Bull in Loring Park near downtown Minneapolis.

Edvard Grieg

With composer Edvard Grieg (1843-1907) and others, there emerged a style of classical composition which often utilized Norwegian folk melodies and rhythms.

Born of musical parents, Grieg was trained musically in the Germanic and Danish traditions. His awakening to the importance of Norwegian music came at age 21 when he spent a summer with the famed violin virtuoso, Ole Bull, who was enthusiastic about the music of his native Norway. He also met Rikard Nordraak, a Norwegian nationalist composer who played and sang some of his own works.

Grieg's musical output from that time included the incidental music for Ibsen's *Peer Gynt,* the Piano Concerto in A minor, many song cycles, character pieces for piano, and chamber music. Grieg achieved international recognition because his style was influenced by the folk melodies, harmonies and rhythms of his native land, in contrast to the Germanic tradition on the continent.

Rikard Nordraak (1842-1866), who died tragically young, composed *"Ja, vi elsker dette landet"* ("Yes, We Love Our Native Land") with words by Bjørnstjerne Bjørnson. It was first performed in May, 1864, in celebration of the 50th anniversary of Norway's constitution.

In America

In America, love of music motivates the popular male choruses and other musical groups for which the immigrant communities have been long noted. Simple folk songs from Norway have been sung by immigrant mothers as they rocked the cradle, and at house parties and community gatherings with accompaniment by fiddlers, accordionists, guitar players and others.

The love of old-time Norwegian music has never died. An annual festival of music has been held at Decorah in connection with the Nordic Fest the last full weekend of July. Other immigrant communities also have musical festivals at which the old-time songs and dances are performed.

Since recording began, the immigrants have had their favorite recording artists keeping alive their music, and each year brings new recordings of Norwegian ethnic music. Recent favorites among recording artists are Else and Mike Sevig, who live in Minneapolis, where Mike is a public school teacher. Their oldest daughter Mari recently made her recording debut with "Just a Little Lefse" on her parents' record, "Scandinavian Smorgasbord."

The Sevigs, like a number of performers, have their own recording firm,

Skandisk Music, 3424 South 19th Avenue, Minneapolis, MN 55407. A similar firm, Banjar Records, Inc., Box 32164, 7440 University Avenue NE, Minneapolis, MN 55432, concentrates on instrumental old-time music.

Song of Norway

On the last Saturday in June and every Saturday in July, the people of the Mt. Horeb, Wisconsin, area stage the famous musical based on the life of Norwegian composer Edvard Grieg.

The musical is performed on the greens of The Cave of The Mounds, Blue Mounds, Wisconsin. Norwegian arts, crafts, foods and direct imports are available in the area throughout the Song of Norway festival.

Norwegian Sculptor

Sculptor Jacob Fjelde (1856-1896), born in Aalesund, Norway, came to Minneapolis in 1887. He is noted for sculptures of Ole Bull, right, in Loring Park, of Hiawatha, left, in Minnehaha Park, and of the Minerva figure in the public library, all in Minneapolis. His sisters were artists in embroidery work and tapestry

weaving. His son, Paul, created the Lincoln monument in Frogner Park in Oslo, Norway, and the statue of Col. Hans C. Heg, commander of the Fifteenth Wisconsin regiment during the Civil War in Lier, Norway. Replicas of the Heg sculpture are in Capitol Park, Madison, Wis., and in Heg Park near Racine, Wis.

(From My Minneapolis *by Carl G.O. Hansen, 1956)*

Thirteen Generations

Their names, for 13 generations we can trace, were: Belest Lauvsnes, Belest Belestson Lauvsnes, Belest Belestson, Roald Belestson, Belest Roaldson, Roald Belestson, Eli Roald, Byre Roald (who married Ola Olsson), Roald Olsson, Belest Roalson (who emigrated to America), Oscar Roalson, John Roalson, and our children—Eric, Brad and Craig Roalson.

Actually the man who emigrated to America was Belest Byröe of the Island of Byröe, near Fister, Norway. Belest's ancestors had lived on this island for at least 10 generations. Belest Byröe married Martha Oledatter of Suldahl. Both were 28 when they came to America.

In America, people had difficulty pronouncing Byröe, so Belest followed the Norwegian custom of adding "son" to his father's name. He became Belest Roaldson, but the "d" was soon dropped.

Belest died of cancer at age 42, Martha died in 1932 at age 88 and was survived by seven children and 31 grandchildren, one of whom is my husband, John.

—Louise Roalson

"The Letter"

They came "because of the letter." It was from their son, Sven Svenson, at Decorah, Iowa. They would need him; none of them knew a word of English. But when Gunnel Svenson and his family arrived at Decorah, they learned that Sven had enlisted in the Union Army and had been killed at Gettysburg.

"Gunnel" translated into English as Gunder, and the place they settled near Decorah became known as Gunder, Iowa.

Great-great-grandfather was buried at the Lutheran Cemetery at Gunder as "Gunnel Svenson Korsgaard," the latter for their farm home in Norway. But except for Rachel Gunderson Korsgaard, the children all took the name Gunderson.

The boys were Knute and Peter Gunderson. By marriage, three girls became Aanestad, Ellings, and Skarshaug. My great-grandmother chose, not the Norwegian youth her father liked, but a Swiss named John Lang. She knew no German and he knew no Norwegian, so they learned English together. They bought land near Remsen in northwest Iowa, and enjoyed a long and happy life.

Samuel Lang, their son, married Eva Penfield. Their daughter, Esther Lang Liffring, is my mother.

—Joan Liffring-Zug,
publisher of Penfield Press

Genealogy

Norwegians in America have great interest in tracing their ancestry. It also works the other way as Norwegians search for their American relatives.

Now help is coming from the Norwegian government, which is subsidizing histories of each family farm in a particular district. Births, deaths, marriages and often dates of emigration are published in book form.

For anyone interested in Norse-American genealogy, one of the best places to contact is the Vesterheim Genealogical Center, c/o Prof. Gerhard B. Naeseth, 4909 Sherwood Road, Madison, Wis., 53711. Include return postage. Prof. Naeseth is a prominent scholar of earlier Norwegian immigration.

To become a member of the Center and subscribe to the periodical, *Norwegian Tracks,* apply to the Norwegian-American Museum, 502 W. Water Street, Decorah, Iowa, 52101.

The library of the Genealogical Society of Utah has film copies of the main genealogical records in Norway and also of American immigration records. The address is 50 East North Temple, Salt Lake City, Utah 84150.

Another source is the Norwegian-American Historical Association housed in the Rölvaag Library of St. Olaf College, Northfield, Minn., 55057.

Additional information on how to proceed can be obtained from Sons of Norway, 1455 West Lake Street, Minneapolis, Minn., 55408.

Giants and Names

There were giants in the earth in those days; and also after that, when the sons of God came in unto the daughters of men, and they bare children to them, the same became mighty men which were of old, men of renown. Genesis vi:4

The ticket had come from his Uncle Jakob, who lived near Elk Point, S.D. At age 20, Ole Edvart Rölvaag accepted the challenge and welcomed the opportunity. He left behind all that was familiar—his homeland in Lofoten in the district of Helgeland, just below the Arctic Circle.

In America, he did farm work in South Dakota, studied at St. Olaf College, Northfield, Minn., and, back in his native land, at the University of Oslo.

From 1906 until his death in 1931, Rölvaag taught Norwegian literature at St. Olaf College. He also found time to create one of the masterpieces of American literature, *Giants in the Earth,* published in Norway in 1924, and translated into English and published in America in 1927 by Harper & Brothers, now Harper & Row.

Giants in the Earth is must reading, not only for persons of Norwegian descent, but for all who would relive the many trials and triumphs of the hard wagon journey westward, the problems of the "great settling," and the heart-rending anxieties of decisions inescapable in accommodating to a land that was at once so strange and so full of hope.

Here we quote, not from the story, but from explanations of terms and names. In the preface of the 1964 Torchbook Edition of the Rölvaag novel, Einar Haugen, the distinguished scholar who is Professor of Scandinavian and Linguistics, Emeritus, at Harvard University, wrote:

The word which is here translated as "settling" or "land-taking" is the Old Norse landnam, *a standard term for the settlement of Iceland by Norwegian Vikings in the ninth century. The proud chieftains who left Norway for the west a thousand years earlier form a romantic backdrop to the humble settlers of our own time.*

In a footnote about names, Rölvaag wrote:

The practice of changing surnames has gone on extensively with the Norwegian-American. Among the common folk in Norway it is quite customary even yet for the son to take his surname from his father's first name; the son of Hans must be Hansen or Hanson. Likewise the girl; if she is the daughter of Hans, her surname becomes Hansdatter (Hans' daughter), which she retains even after marriage. When the Norwegians became independent landowners in America their slumbering sense of the historical fitness of things awoke, and so many of them adopted the name of the place they had come from in the old country. Hence the many American names now ending in —dahl, —fjeld, —gaard, —stad, etc. As the Swedes, and the Danes, too, had so many Hansens and Olsens and Johnsons, the change was really a very practical one.

O.E. Rölvaag: Giants in the Earth, *1964, Torchbook Edition, courtesy Harper & Row, Publishers, Inc., New York.*

Early Americans

There were Norwegians and Danes among the Dutch who founded New Amsterdam, which became New York City.

That was in the 1600s, and in those days, Norway was under the Danish king. Norwegian seamen served in both the Danish navy and merchant marine, but there were a great many Norwegian seamen sailing for the Dutch, who at that time were expanding Dutch influence worldwide.

The May parade in Brooklyn, New York, attracts over 50,000 viewers and has costumed Norwegians and floats representing churches, schools and Norse organizations. *Photographs from Sigurd Daasvand, Nordisk Tidende.*

Norwegians in New York

For many Norwegians coming to the United States, New York City was the port of entry. For some, the journey had been long enough and they were ready to call New York home.

Today more than 50,000 Norwegians live in the four New York City boroughs, Long Island and New Jersey. The Bay Ridge section of Brooklyn is the heart of the New York Norwegian community.

Three churches conduct services in the Norwegian language. In addition to Sunday services, meetings are held Thursdays and Saturdays. The churches are Trinity Lutheran Church at 46th Street and 4th Avenue, Lutheran Brethren Free Church at 59th Street and 8th Avenue and First Evangelical Free Church at 66th Street and 6th Avenue.

The highlight of the year is the annual parade the first Sunday after May 17 to celebrate Norwegian Independence Day. The grandstand is in Leif Erikson Park in Bay Ridge. About 20 bands participate, sometimes including a band from Norway.

Fifth and Eighth Avenues in Brooklyn are still dotted with Norwegian shops and services—delicatessans, gift shops, restaurants, bakeries, butcher shops, a funeral parlor and other businesses.

Colleges

Colleges founded by Norwegian-American Lutherans are: Augustana College, Sioux Falls, S.D., Luther College, Decorah, Iowa, Augsburg College, Minneapolis, Minn., St. Olaf College, Northfield, Minn., Wagner College, New York City, Pacific Lutheran University, Tacoma, Wash., Concordia College, Moorhead, Minn., Lutheran Theological Seminary, St. Paul Minn., and California Lutheran College, Thousand Oaks. Calif. Many have annual celebrations of their Norwegian heritage.

Newspapers

Between 1865 and 1914 there were 565 newspapers and magazines in the United States printed in the Norwegian language. Today there are two: *The Western Viking* of Seattle and *Nordisk Tidende* of Brooklyn, plus one that is in English, *Vinland* of Evanston, Ill.

Minnesota Norwegians

More first, second and third generation Norwegians live in Minnesota than in any other state.

Norwegians in Texas

In 1971 the University of Texas Institute of Texan Cultures at San Antonio published a booklet titled *The Norwegian Texans* tracing the history of the Norwegians who settled in Texas.

The first Norwegian settler was Johan Nordboe, self-taught painter and physician, who moved from the Fox River, Illinois, settlement of the Sloopers to a farm in Dallas County, Texas, between 1837 and 1841.

Henderson County, Texas, was the site of the first Norwegian settlement, called Normandy and later Brownsboro. It was founded by Johan Reinert Reiersen and his family. Like Norway, the landscape had high ridges and pine woods. A second settlement, called Four Mile Prairie, was founded by Reiersen on the border of Kaufman and Van Zandt Counties in 1848 when the Texas government offered 640 acres free to families, 320 acres free to single men.

In 1849 Cleng Peerson, who founded the Fox River settlement, visited John Nordboe. Upon returning to Illinois, he urged Norwegians coming to America to move to Texas instead of the upper Midwest or Canada.

When the Texas legislature created Bosque County in 1854, Cleng Peerson urged Norwegians to move into the area for better soil, water and wood supplies. The southwest part of Bosque County is the most Norwegian area of Texas. Stone houses of the pioneers are landmarks.

Other descendants of Norwegians in Texas are wheat farmers in Hansford County of the northern Texas panhandle.

The Mother Language

Courses in Norwegian are offered by most of the colleges founded by Norwegian immigrants, and state universities in Minnesota, Wisconsin and Washington have had strong programs in Scandinavian studies with considerable emphasis on Norwegian.

Adult education programs and youth language camps carry on the tradition of instruction in the ethnic languages. Such national organizations as the Sons of Norway have played a major role in these programs.

International Language Villages is a summer camp program sponsored by Concordia College, Moorhead, Minn. 56560. Since its start in 1961, enrollment has grown to more than 2,000 each summer, with about 700 in Skogfjorden, a 17th century Norwegian village on Turtle River Lake north of Bemidji, Minn.

Other languages taught in villages that simulate Old World environments are German, French, Spanish, Russian, Swedish, Finnish and Danish. Children and teenagers are enrolled.

Enthusiastic support for this program has come from the Parents Advisory Council; from individuals such as Mr. and Mrs. Ed Fish and Mr. and Mrs. Don Padilla of Minneapolis; from organizations including Lutheran Brotherhood, Edyth Bush Charitable Foundation, the Salolampi Foundation, Friends of Sjolunden, American Swedish Institute, Vasa Order of America and others. Districts I and IV Sons of Norway offer more than 300 scholarships totaling $40,000 a year.

Organized programs for the study of Norwegian in Norway also are common. One is sponsored by the Norwegian-American Cultural Institute of the Twin Cities in Minnesota. The Oslo International Summer School has an American office at St. Olaf College, Northfield, Minn., and recruits many of its students from the Norwegian-American community.

The Norwegian-American Museum

Over 12,000 items in the collection of the Norwegian-American Museum, Decorah, Iowa, graphically tell a story of Norwegian immigration in three chapters: life in Norway, the immigrant voyages, and life in America.

Visitors see exhibits depicting domestic and rural life in Norway more than a century ago, and then enter the Westby Ship Gallery with its story of Atlantic crossings. The gallery's 40-foot height easily accommodates the single-masted, 24-foot *Tradewind,* built by two Norwegian brothers who sailed it to the 1933 World's Fair at Chicago. Nearby is a model of the *Restoration,* a sloop which brought the 53 immigrants to America in 1825. It was little more than twice the length of the *Tradewind.*

Exhibits of the life of immigrants in America include a log cabin built from a single pine tree and furnished with simple pieces made of planks. There are axes of the pioneers and what they made with them, including wood shovels and a wagon with solid wheels hewed from a log.

Such exhibits tell their story of hardship, toil and purpose. In contrast are bright and happy associations of folk art —colorful wall hangings, intricate costumes, embroideries, a hand-carved altarpiece, a beautiful bridal crown, and exhibits of rosemaling, silver, china, glass and many others.

The museum, known as *Vesterheim* (home in the west), traces its beginnings from 1877, when Luther College of Decorah, which had been established by immigrants from Norway, began receiving and collecting items relating to Norwegian immigration.

Knut Gjerset, professor of history at Luther, actively expanded the collection, and in 1933 obtained the recently vacated building of the Lutheran Publishing House, which still serves as the central museum building.

The museum is one of the first in this country to introduce the folk museum concept which, according to its director, Marion Nelson, "differs from the usual museum in placing its emphasis on the common man and in concerning itself with total outdoor environments as well as with individual objects."

Historic buildings, including two from Norway, are part of the Vesterheim complex. The museum is open daily.

Nordic Heritage Museum

Founded in 1979, the Nordic Heritage Museum of Seattle is developing a collection that tells the story of Scandinavian immigrants in the Pacific Northwest and the merging of their traditions and customs with the American culture. Artifacts on display include skis donated by the Norwegian Ski Museum in Oslo.

The museum has hosted exhibits and programs featuring weaving, rosemaling, wood carving, folk music, dance and lectures. Marianne Forssblad is museum director. The museum is in a former school building at 3014 N.W. 67th Street in Seattle, Washington, 98117.

The Norsk Museum

The Sloopers, who arrived in the United States in 1825, settled the Fox River Valley in Illinois in 1834. It was five years before they were joined by a lay minister. He was Elling **Eielsen,** who was born in Voss, Norway, in 1804.

The church building which is now the Norsk Museum was built in 1849 by his congregation. The museum is dedicated "to the memory of the Rev. Elling Eielsen, first Norwegian Lutheran pastor in America."

The village of Norway is on the Cleng Peerson Memorial Highway (No. 71). It is the site of the Norsk Museum, the Cleng Peerson Memorial Park, the J. Hart Rosdail Memorial and the National Norwegian-American Memorial, an outdoor board that tells the "Norsk Story."

Vesterheim Landmarks

More than 200 landmarks of interest to Norwegian-Americans have been registered by the Vesterheim Landmarks Committee since it began its research in 1974. Rolf Erickson of Evanston, Ill., heads the committee.

The "Vesterheim Landmark" listing includes significant collections of artifacts such as the collections at Vesterheim in Decorah, Iowa, and at Little Norway in Mt. Horeb, Wis.; the Stoughton (Wis.) Historical Society Collection; and the collections of the Olmstead County Historical Society in Rochester, Minn.

Examples of other types of landmarks that have been registered are:

—The Norway Center in Chicago, originally the Chicago Norske Klub, a two-story building at the corner of Kedzie and Fullerton. It was opened July 4, 1917.

—The Koren monument by Sigvald Asbjørnsen, made of bronze medallions affixed to a granite shaft in the Washington Prairie Cemetery seven miles from Decorah, Iowa. It is a monument for Elisabeth and Vilhelm Koren.

—The Berdahl-Rölvaag house, built in 1884 by the Anders Berdahl family 15 miles from Sioux Falls, South Dakota. It is the birthplace of Mr. and Mrs. Berdahl's daughter Jennie Marie, who married novelist O.E. Rölvaag.

—The Leif Ericson statue by Anne Whitney in Boston. It was unveiled Oct. 29, 1887. The inscription reads: "Leif Ericson landed here A.D. 1000."

—Cleng Peerson monument at Norse, Bosque County, Texas. The inscription reads: "Cleng Peerson/The First Norwegian Immigrant/to America/Came to America in 1821/Born in Norway, Europe, May 17, 1782/Died in Texas December 16, 1865/Grateful Countrymen in Texas Erected this/Monument to his Memory."

—Colonel Hans Christian Heg statue in Madison, Wis. Heg was the highest-ranking officer from Wisconsin killed during the Civil War (Sept. 19, 1863).

The Gokstad Ship

From an ancient burial mound in Norway, there was unearthed in 1880 the Gokstad ship, which sailed the seas in the eighth and ninth centuries.

Magnus Andersen saw in this discovery an opportunity to prove that Vikings could have discovered America. He raised funds, built an exact replica of the *Gokstadskip,* and in a 28-day voyage with 12 oarsmen he sailed from Bergen right up to Chicago's lakefront for the 1893 World's Columbian Exposition.

Today this historic ship rests in Lincoln Park, Chicago, in a deteriorated condition. Restoration efforts are being sponsored by the American Scandinavian Foundation, Danish National Committee, Icelandic Association, League of Finnish-American Societies, Norwegian National League and Swedish Central Committee.

Sons of Norway

The Sons of Norway is the largest and most enduring of the Norwegian-American organizations. Founded in Minneapolis in 1896 and modeled after American fraternal lodges, it started as a mutual aid fund and later became a large insurance company with a cultural program. Since 1942, the membership magazine has been printed in English, developing renewed interest in young people. There are approximately 350 lodges in the United States and Canada.

Slooper Society of America

Members are lineal descendants of the Sloopers and their spouses. Visitors are welcome at the annual meeting, held the afternoon of the Sunday nearest to October 9 at the Milton Pope School, 1½ miles east and 4½ miles south of Norway, Ill.

Syttende Mai Minnesota

More than 50 separate organizations are members of Syttende Mai Minnesota and cooperate each year in events celebrating Norway's Constitution Day.

A typical celebration on Saturday, May 15, 1982, included a two-hour parade through downtown Minneapolis, with 80 marching units and hundreds of children carrying Norwegian flags.

There was a full day of demonstrations of Norwegian arts, crafts and cooking; musical programs by choirs, folk-singing groups, accordionists and fiddlers; and displays of costumes, antiques and import products. In the evening, there was a banquet.

The theme of this annual celebration is that Minnesota is the most Norwegian of all the 50 states. But the celebration is only one of many that are held on a suitable date near May 17.

The event celebrated by these Norwegian-Americans occurred on May 17, 1814. Norway had been under Denmark's control for four centuries. Denmark had favored Napoleon; Sweden had opposed him. After Napoleon's defeat, the treaty of Kiel took Norway from Denmark and "gave" it to Sweden.

In response, Norwegians held elections and chose delegates to a Constituent Assembly which on May 17 adopted a Constitution declaring Norway independent. The Assembly elected Prince Christian Frederik as King of Norway. Heir to the Danish throne, the prince—also the King's deputy in Norway—had supported the Norwegian independence movement.

Sweden's response was to send troops into Norway. An armistice was reached August 14, 1814. Under its terms, Prince Christian Frederik abdicated as King of Norway, but Norway remained under its new Constitution while accepting union with Sweden under the King of Sweden. Norway's full independence under its own king was delayed until 1905. Independence came by peaceful means.

Other Syttende Mai celebrations include the following: Ottawa, Ill., Spring Grove, Minn., Brooklyn, N.Y., Seattle and Tacoma, Wash., and Stoughton and Westby, Wis.

Here are some of the other Norwegian-American celebrations:

First Saturday in May—Norwegian Day at Pacific Lutheran University, Tacoma, Wash.

First Weekend in June—Three-day festival at Story City, Iowa—parade, ethnic food, flea market, baseball, band concerts, rosemaling and other events.

June—St. Hans Festival sponsored by Tacoma, Wash., Daughters of Norway.

July—Nordland Fest at Augustana College, Sioux Falls, S.D. Three days with many events—from lectures to rock-throwing contests.

Second Sunday in July—At Minneapolis, Norway Day festivities in Minnehaha Park.

Last weekend in July—Three-day Nordic Fest in Decorah, Iowa. National competitive exhibitions of rosemaling, woodcarving and weaving. Extensive program of music, dancing, crafts, ethnic foods, sports and much more.

October—Annual Festival in Minot, N.D.

St. Hans Day

Throughout Norway, St. Hans Day is celebrated June 24 in observance of the longest day of the year. On St. Hans Eve, the young celebrate with all-night bonfires, singing, dancing and merry-making. In Tacoma, Wash., the Daughters of Norway sponsor a St. Hans festival which includes a program and the serving of *rømmegrøt*.

The Setesdal Room represents the 17th century at Vesterheim. At Christmas time, farm families decorated with straw. The goat's head on the pole served as a noisemaker used to ward off evil spirits which, according to folklore, visited farms and homes during the holiday season. *Darrell Henning photo.*

Christmas Traditions

Christmas traditions in a Norwegian-American home have their roots in faraway times and places and also reflect a melding with American customs.

Some customs can be traced back to pre-Christian pagan times when the Vikings celebrated *jol.* A swine was killed as a sacrifice and the meat used for a feast. Today a pig is killed before Christmas on a typical Norwegian farm to serve during the holidays.

Also part of pagan lore is the *nisse.* On Christmas Eve a bowl of porridge was placed in the barn to appease this gnome so he would not play tricks. This practice continues in some parts of Norway, but with tongue in cheek. In America, the *nisse* is found in the form of a doll, a table decoration or a tree ornament.

To go *julebukk* (pronounced yool-a-book) is a delightful Norwegian custom dating from the Middle Ages. The word means "Christmas goat." Young people wearing strange outfits and carrying a goat's head on a stick went from farm to farm scaring spirits. Some children in Norway still "go *julebukk*" in the same way American children have tricks and treats at Halloween. In America there are *julebukker* in heavily populated Norwegian areas.

It is typical in Norway to put out a sheaf of oats on a pole for the birds. Called *julenek,* this may have started as an offering to the fertility gods. It also reflects the Christian idea of seeing that all God's creatures are well fed at the time of celebrating Christ's birth.

The farm animals were given extra portions at Christmas time.

In Norway, holiday parties are given *after* Christmas, not before as they tend to be in America. Although preparations start weeks before Christmas, the season officially opens with the sounds of church bells ringing all over the country at 6 p.m. Christmas Eve.

To symbolize purity, the foods are white —*lutefisk,* creamed potatoes, *lefse* and rice pudding. A single almond is baked into the pudding. Whoever finds the almond will have good luck for the coming year and may receive a small gift, often a marzipan pig. Sometimes a raisin is also baked in the pudding, and the finder is the loser who has to do the cleanup chores after the meal.

The Christmas tree came to Norway from Germany. The family tree is usually not decorated until a day or two before Christmas. Until recently the tree was decorated by the parents behind closed doors. Traditionally, lights on the tree are all white. Strings of tiny Norwegian flags are part of the decorations. A star tops the tree.

Each ship at sea has its own lighted tree tied to the mast.

During World War II King Haakon VII took refuge in London while the Germans occupied Norway. Every Christmas his subjects sent a Norway spruce to him. Ever since, Norway sends a huge tree each Christmas to stand in Trafalgar Square.

Baking is a big part of Christmas preparations for those of Norwegian background. Popular confections are *sandbakkels, fattigmann, rosettes, kringle, spritz* and *Berlinerkranser.* Another must is *julekake,* a sweet yeast bread full of raisins, currants and citron.

In a flurry of preparations at least 14 different kinds of cookies or cakes had to be baked in Norway, one for each day of the holiday season. Today, seven will suffice and some homemakers purchase the goodies from the bakery.

In Norway, *Juledag,* First Christmas Day, starts with a church service. The day is devoted to family. On Second Christmas Day, the rounds of visits to family and friends begin. This continues for several days.

Some Norwegians have had enough holiday by *Nyttårsdag* (New Year's Day). Others stretch the good times until Jan. 6 (Epiphany or Twelfth Night). For others, festivities continue until Jan. 13 (20th Day), which is a feast day for St. Canute. The saying goes "Twentieth Day Canute drives Christmas away."

In Norway, they like to say *"Gledelig Jul!"* or *"God Jul!"* as long and as often as possible.

Norwegian Foods

Fish, fish and more fish. Reindeer meat. Boiled potatoes served with every dinner. Herring, cheese and sliced tomatoes for breakfast. Coffee breaks with lavish spreads of layered cakes and crisp cookies. A swallow of the native aquavit that burns all the way down.

These are among my culinary memories of a visit to Norway. On a three-day bus tour between Oslo and Bergen, the rousing strains of a Grieg concerto burst from the sound system of the bus. Daily fresh flowers were on the console between Knute the driver and Bjorn the tour director. Craggy mountains, quiet lakes, clear mountain streams, tumultuous waterfalls, ungainly goats, red-cheeked children and 11th century stave churches —all these are beautiful and not at all like America.

Why would my husband's grandparents leave such a beautiful country for the mid-

American plains? Certainly not for the scenery.

But leave it they did in 1872 with their six-month-old baby Roal. Belest and Martha, both 28, packed their belongings, took a sailboat to Quebec, a train to Milwaukee and an ox-drawn covered wagon to Iowa. They settled near Ossian in Winneshiek County in northeast Iowa. In 1876 they moved to the north central Iowa area of Thor, Humboldt County, where they bought a farm and built a sod house.

Belest and Martha banded together with other Norwegians to forge ties and friendships with those of like backgrounds. They shared the good times and the bad. Knowing little English, they clung to Norwegian ways but the New World meant adapting to new foods.

Pork was one food that took some getting used to. In Norway it had been only a Christmas treat. Here, every farmer seemed to have plenty of pigs to slaughter. Bacon was something they had not been accustomed to eating.

Grøt was a favorite food. This hearty porridge made by boiling milk with flour was the main dish for many a pioneer meal. Its Norwegian origin goes back to ancient times. If rich cream is used instead of milk, it becomes *rømmegrøt*, which is considered a treat in Norwegian homes today.

Meat was not plentiful. Stews, soups, and meatballs were used to stretch what meat was available. These were (and are) delicious. When there was lamb there was *får i kål* (lamb and cabbage). This simple stew is popular in Norway.

They missed the salt-water fish of their homeland—the cod, salmon, herring and mackerel. Dried foods were not as common in America, either, so they seldom fixed *lutefisk*, which calls for dried cod.

Fish from Iowa streams were boiled and served with melted butter. Or they ended up in *fiskesuppe* (fish soup), *fiskeboller,* (fish balls) or *fiskepudding* (a baked mixture of flaked fish and cream sauce). Today *fiskeboller* can be bought canned and *fiskepudding* remains popular in Norway, where it is served in some households once a week.

There were boiled potatoes with meals. and dumplings were common. Potatoes were a base for *lefse,* a bread that is rolled thin and baked on a grill.

As in Norway, the immigrants favored root vegetables that kept well over the winter. They grew carrots, cabbage, beets, onions, turnips and rutabagas.

They didn't bother much with salads. Pickled beets or pickled cucumbers were considered salad enough, and still are in some Norwegian homes.

Fruits appeared on the table in the form of fruit soup, or sweet soup. This dish is far from ordinary soups. It is a mixture of fresh or dried fruits cooked with a thickening of tapioca. Into it goes whatever fruits are available—apples, plums, berries, cherries, peaches and currants, for example. For the lingonberries (*tyttebær*) of Norway, these newcomers substituted the berries of America.

Of course they baked bread, using wheat and rye flour. In addition to the unleavened flatbread (*flatbrød*) they were used to, they now made yeast breads, too.

For dessert there was *rødgrøt*, red fruit pudding made from red fruit juices, a sort of junket, plus various cakes and cookies. *Tilslørte bondepiker* (veiled peasant girls) was layered, buttered and toasted bread crumbs, thickened fruit and whipped "real" cream.

Special occasions called for special recipes—and still do. *Eggedosis* to celebrate Norway's Constitution Day May 17 is easy to make, needing only beaten eggs and sugar.

Kransekake, the national cake of Norway, was created to celebrate weddings, christenings, anniversaries and birthdays. These concentric rings of almond-flavored cakes sometimes reach a height of two feet.

Today, among the fourth and fifth generation Norwegians, there is an upsurge of interest in the Norwegian heritage, much of it involving food traditions. Making and serving dishes like those described in this little book is a delicious way of participating.

—Louise Roalson

19

Main Dishes

Meatballs
Norma's kjøttboller

Norma Anderson Wangsness of Decorah, Iowa, says "this is our all-time family favorite and always made for Christmas Eve supper. The rest of the menu includes lutefisk, mashed potatoes, baked mashed rutabagas, lefse, flatbread, scalloped corn, a Christmas salad of red and green gelatin or a 24-hour salad, rømmegrøt and spritz cookies."

Meatballs:
- 2 quarts water
- 1 medium onion, chopped
- few stalks celery, finely chopped
- 1½ lbs. ground round steak or meatball mix of pork, beef and veal (preferably unseasoned)
- 1 cup cream
- 1 egg
- 1 Tbsp. cornstarch
- salt and pepper (salt optional because of soups used in gravy)

Gravy:
- 2 cans consommé
- 1 can cream of mushroom soup
- 3 Tbsp. flour

Heat water, onion and celery in deep kettle. Mix meatball ingredients well and form into balls. When water boils, drop meatballs into liquid and simmer until they hold their shapes. Remove from broth and put meatballs into a baking dish sprayed with vegetable spray. Cover meatballs with soups mixed with flour. Bake at 350 degrees F. covered for one hour. Uncover and bake ½ hour more to brown.

"This can be prepared and frozen before baking. Thaw and bake. I usually do 10 pounds of meatball mixture at a time and freeze several assorted size casseroles so I always have spare for unexpected company. For that amount of meat, use 4 cups cream, 7 or 8 eggs, 6 to 8 tablespoons cornstarch, 8 cans of consommé, 8 cans of mushroom soup and 1 cup flour."

Norwegian Meatballs
Kjøttboller

Olivia Vik Hendrickson of Decorah, Iowa, writes: "I grew up in a large family where much food was prepared. Through the years there were times when the budget couldn't include steaks, etc., so this was what we made instead.

"Having been a teacher and the wife of a school administrator, I have done a great deal of entertaining. These meatballs go well with new peas and potatoes as well as with potato salad. Once the meat is ready, you can entertain at the drop of a hat."

- 1 lb. lean pork
- 1 lb. lean beef
- 2 large potatoes, boiled and mashed or 1 cup instant potatoes prepared with 1 cup boiling water
- 2 eggs
- 1 cup milk
- 1 small onion, finely chopped

Grind meat finely. (I have my butcher put it through the grinder three times.) Mix all ingredients well. Shape into rolls the size of an egg. Dip balls in flour. Fry in butter or margarine. Put in a 13x9 pan. Rinse skillet with 1½ cups water. Pour over meatballs. Bake at 325 degrees F. for 40 minutes. Turn down temperature to 300 degrees for an additional 20 minutes.

"This will serve six generously. These meatballs freeze well, so can be made ahead. I usually double the recipe. They are a good gift."

No Need to Row

Ole Evinrude, a Norse immigrant who grew up on a Wisconsin farm, invented the first practical outboard motor.

Meatballs
Kjøttboller

This recipe is used at the First Lutheran Church Smorgasbord for the Nordic Fest in Decorah, Iowa. Notice that no onions are used. According to Norma Wangsness of Decorah, "A real Norwegian never puts onions in meatballs. The consommé and mushroom soup are present-day additions. Also, evaporated milk is substituted for cream as the old-fashioned 'from the farm' cream is not possible to get. For Nordic Fest, the ladies of the Circle would each make a 10-pound batch and deliver it to the church ready to serve. Now they gather at church to make all that will be needed and each lady takes some home to freeze and return at Nordic Fest time."

5 lbs. beef, pork and veal, finely ground
salt optional
1 tsp. dry mustard
1 tsp. mace
1 tsp. pepper
1½ 13-oz. cans evaporated milk
1 can consommé
1 can mushroom soup

Mix meat, salt, mustard, mace, pepper and milk. Form into balls. Brown in butter. Add mixture of soups. Simmer briefly. Place in casserole and bake at 350 degrees F. for 1 hour.

The Kon-Tiki Raft

Norwegian Thor Heyerdahl and five companions sailed on the balsa-wood raft Kon-Tiki from Peru to the Tuanota Islands in eastern Polynesia, seeking to demonstrate that the islands could have been settled by Indians from America. *Kon-Tiki*, his book about the voyage, was published in 1950. Later, he wrote two other books: *Aku-Aku*, about Easter Island, and *Fatu-Hiva*, or "Back to Nature."

Royal Pot Roast
Slottsstek

Verla Williams of Iowa City, Iowa.

2 Tbsp. butter
2 Tbsp. vegetable oil
4 lbs. boneless beef (round, rump or chuck)
1 cup finely chopped onion
3 Tbsp. flour
1 Tbsp. dark corn syrup
2 Tbsp. white vinegar
2 cups beef stock
1 large bay leaf
6 flat anchovy fillets, washed and drained
1 tsp. whole peppercorns, crushed and tied in cheesecloth
salt
black pepper, freshly ground

In heavy 5- to 6-quart oven-proof casserole melt butter and oil over moderate heat. When foam subsides, brown meat on all sides, taking about 15 minutes. Remove meat from pan. Add onion and cook over moderately high heat 6 to 8 minutes, stirring occasionally until lightly browned. Remove pan from heat. Add flour. Stir gently to blend. Add dark syrup, white vinegar and stock. Add bay leaf, anchovies and bag of peppercorns. Replace meat, cover and bring to boil on top of stove. Preheat oven to 350 degrees F. Place casserole on shelf in lower third of oven, regulating heat so liquid barely simmers. Meat should be tender in about 3 hours.

Transfer roast to heated platter. Cover with foil to keep warm. Discard bay leaf and peppercorns. Skim off surface fat. Taste and add salt and pepper if necessary. If flavor is lacking, boil briskly, uncovered, over high heat to concentrate. Pour in gravy boat and serve with meat.

"In Scandinavia, *slottsstek* is usually accompanied by red currant jelly or lingonberries, and often with gherkins and boiled potatoes."

Pressed Sandwich Meat
Rullepølse

Barbara Hawes of Grand Rapids, Mich., writes, "This meat roll recipe was given to me by my Norwegian friends, William and Birdene Amundson of Grand Rapids, who formerly lived in Stoughton, Wis. It is a challenge to make, but worth it." Barbara's interests include rosemaling, cooking and quilting.

2½ lbs. beef flank
1 Tbsp. pepper
4 tsp. salt
2 tsp. ginger
½ tsp. sugar
1 lb. thinly sliced beef from the round
½ lb. sliced pork tenderloin
¼ lb. finely ground pork
¼ lb. finely ground beef
3 Tbsp. minced onion

Trim all fat from flank. Flatten with meat pounder on a board. Mix seasonings, spice and sugar. Rub part of mixture into flank. Place sliced beef and pork on half of flank. Combine ground beef and pork with remaining seasonings and onion. Spread over beef and pork slices.

Roll meat tightly; sew together with strong thread. Wrap tightly in a piece of cheesecloth. Put in a heavy kettle and cover with water. Simmer for 2½ to 3 hours until tender.

Remove from kettle. Place roll between two heavy plates under a heavy weight to press out moisture. Keep in cool place several hours or overnight. Remove cloth and thread. Refrigerate.

Serve cold, cut in thin slices. Makes 10 to 12 servings. Can be made ahead. "A fine addition to a buffet menu."

Eric Sevareid

Eric Sevareid, a well-known news correspondent, was born in North Dakota, attended the University of Minnesota, and joined CBS in 1939. He is of Norwegian descent.

Norwegian Taco
Lefsekling

Eunice Stoen of Decorah sent this recipe. She says: "This was the result of trying to come up with a unique food to serve during Decorah's Nordic Fest. My good friend Ida Sacquitne tells us her grandmother called it lefsekling whenever they wrapped whatever they had to eat in lefse. Most Norwegians don't like too hot a sauce, so we mixed one part of the mild taco sauce to two parts catsup."

Meat mixture:
butter
chopped onion
ground beef
salt and pepper
3 to 4 Tbsp. brown sugar
chicken gumbo soup
Filling ingredients:
shredded head lettuce
chopped tomatoes
white cheese, shredded in food processor
chopped onions
mild sauce, 2 parts catsup to 1 part taco sauce
lefse (about 9" size)

Brown onion in butter; add beef and brown. Add salt and pepper to taste, a little brown sugar and ½ to 1 can chicken gumbo soup, depending on amount of meat. Simmer and keep warm for serving.

To serve: With the lefse as the base, put handful of lettuce on top, then 2 or 3 tablespoons meat, tomatoes, cheese, onion and sauce. Fold up and, then fold in sides and then fold the top down and serve in square of foil, along with 2 or 3 paper napkins. *"Very tasty, but messy to eat."*

Make small 9-inch lefse for this recipe. About 1/6 cup dough will make that size.

Remoulade Sandwich
Rulade smørbrød

The recipe for this sandwich, served at the Nordic Brunch and dinner, comes from Berit Gjerde of Edina, Minn. The two meals are sponsored annually by the Twin Cities Friends of the Norwegian-American Museum.

For each sandwich, stack in the following order:

- 1 **well-buttered slice whole wheat bread**
- 1 **leaf Bibb lettuce washed, dried and pressed down**
- 2 **slices roast beef, placed flat with an overlapped twist**
- 2 **Tbsp. chopped soft fried onion, tucked under rounded form of beef slices**
- 1½ **Tbsp. Remoulade sauce**
- 3 **slices pickled beets**
- 1 **tsp. parsley, snipped and sprinkled over surface**
- 3 **thin cucumber slices, cut and twisted to crown top**

Remoulade Sauce:
- 1 **egg**
- 1 **Tbsp. lemon juice**
- ¾ **tsp. salt**
- ½ **tsp. dry mustard**
- ¼ **tsp. paprika**
- ⅛ **tsp. ground white pepper**
- 1 **cup salad oil, divided**
- 1 **Tbsp. lemon juice**
- ½ **tsp. garlic salt**
- 2 **tsp. anchovy paste**
- 1 **sprig parsley**
- 4 **stuffed green olives**
- 1 **tsp. chervil**

Have all ingredients at room temperature. Put egg, the first tablespoon lemon juice, salt, dry mustard, paprika and pepper into blender. Cover and run on low speed. While blender is running, slowly pour in ½ cup salad oil.

When more power is needed, turn speed to high and add second tablespoon lemon juice. Slowly add remaining half cup salad oil.

If the mixture separates, pour it into bowl. Wash and dry blender container. Break one egg into container, cover and run on low speed. While blender is running slowly, add the separated mixture until it is the desired thickness.

Add garlic salt, anchovy paste, parsley, green olives and chervil. Blend. Refrigerate until ready to use. Makes 1¼ cups, enough for 16 sandwiches.

Kirsten Flagstad's Favorite Sandwich

Opera lovers for many years enjoyed Kirsten Flagstad through the Metropolitan Opera radio broadcasts. Born in 1895, she came from a musical family and made her debut in the Oslo National Theatre at age 18. She was known for her Wagnerian roles as Brunnhilde and Isolde. In 1959, she was a founder and the first director of the Norway Opera in Oslo. This recipe is reprinted with permission from Forlaget Tanum-Norli A/S of Oslo, publisher of Norway's Delight *by Elise Sverdup.*

- ½ **ox kidney**
- **flour**
- **salt and pepper**
- **butter**
- 1 **cup cream**
- 1 **glass sherry**
- 4 **slices milk loaf**
- **celeriac**
- **baked apple**
- **tomato and parsley for garnish**

Cut up kidney into small cubes; dust with flour, salt and pepper and brown in butter. Add cream and sherry and simmer for 5 minutes.

Remove crusts from four slices of milk loaf and fry in butter. Place one round lightly boiled disc of celeriac on each slice, then a warm, thick slice of baked apple. Spoon the kidney on top of each loaf and garnish with tomato and parsley. Serves 4.

Pork Sandwich Filling
Flesk pålegg

Esther M. Johnson, Ossian, Iowa, writes: "My mother's maiden name was Stena Tofte Anderson. Tofte, Minn., on Lake Superior, was named for my grandfather and his brother.

"Later my grandfather came south to Dover township, Fayette County, Iowa. Taking his father's first name which was Anders and adding on, it became Anderson, so he went by Hans Tofte Anderson."

3- to 4-lb. pork roast
2 medium onions
1 10½-oz. can cream of chicken soup

Boil roast in unsalted water until tender. Grind with onions. Mix with soup. If the roast is large, two cans of soup may be needed.

This will make enough filling for at least 2 dozen double sandwiches. Freezes well.

Norwegian Stew
Lapskaus

Josefa Hansen Andersen of Chicago, Ill., writes that in Chicago this is often served on May 17, Norway's Independence Day. "At one time," she says, "there were more than 40 churches in Chicago with services in Norwegian, but now there is only one." That is her church, the Norwegian Lutheran Memorial Church, 2612 North Kedzie Boulevard.

1½ cups diced uncooked beef
½ cup diced uncooked pork
1 onion, diced
1½ cups diced cooked corned beef
4 cups diced raw potatoes
½ tsp. pepper

Cover beef and pork with water and boil slowly for half an hour. Add remaining ingredients and cook until tender.

Muriel Humphrey's Beef Soup
Kjøttsuppe

Muriel Humphrey Brown of Waverly, Minn., was the wife of the late Hubert Humphrey, vice-president of the United States from 1965-1969. She says: "This is a hearty old family recipe my father used to make and was Hubert's favorite. He liked to tell everyone it gave him vim, vigor and vitality. Makes six good, hearty bowls."

1½ lbs. stew beef or chuck plus soup bone
1 tsp. salt
½ tsp. pepper
2 bay leaves
4 or 5 medium carrots, sliced
½ cup chopped onion
1 cup chopped celery
1 cup chopped cabbage
1 1-lb. can Italian-style tomatoes
1 Tbsp. Worcestershire sauce
1 beef bouillon cube
pinch oregano or other spice

Cover meat with cold water in heavy 3-quart kettle. Add salt, pepper and bay leaves. Bring to bubbly stage while preparing vegetables. Turn heat low and add carrot, onion, celery and cabbage. Simmer at least 2½ hours or until meat is very tender.

Remove bone and bay leaves. Cut meat into bite-sized pieces. Add tomatoes, Worcestershire sauce and bouillon cube. Simmer for ½ hour longer and serve.

"This recipe is especially good for a light supper meal with fruit salad, a glass of milk, lots of crackers and dessert. It is low in calories, but high in food value."

The Cyclotron

For inventing the cyclotron, Ernest O. Lawrence was awarded the Nobel Prize in Physics in 1939. The cyclotron is "an accelerator in which particles move in a spiral path under the influence of alternating voltage and a magnetic field." Lawrence was born in Canton, S.D.

Containers for all imaginable household purposes were created of birchroot. The small object is for lump sugar. The large baskets were for carrying circular flatbread. The simple covered basket (center, back) came to this country with the family of Knute Nelson, renowned governor and senator of Minnesota at the beginning of the 20th century. Vesterheim collection.

Potato Dumplings and Roast Pork
Kumla med svinesteik

Marilyn Skaugstad of Iowa City, Iowa.

4- to 5-lb. pork roast
Dumplings:
    5 lbs. raw potatoes, peeled and grated
    1 Tbsp. salt
    2 to 2½ cups flour

Cook pork roast in salted water for about two hours to make tasty broth. Grate potatoes and drain excess moisture. Add salt and two cups flour to make dumpling dough. Mix well and test a tablespoon of dough in slowly boiling broth. If it falls apart, add another ½ cup flour to dough and test again until it stays together. Drop gently by large tablespoons into the slowly boiling broth. Dip spoon in broth between dumplings. Cover and cook about 1 to 1½ hours. Occasionally shake pan to prevent sticking to bottom of pan. Serve hot with butter to accompany the pork roast. Makes about 16 large dumplings.

Salt Pork (Side Pork) and Gravy
Sideflesk

Dagny Stenehjem Padilla, Minnetonka, Minn., writes: "My great-great-grandparents and great-grandparents used this recipe for a hearty breakfast when they pioneered southeastern Minnesota in 1849. My folks used it occasionally when I was growing up. It's an economical and filling meal."

    1 lb. side pork, sliced
    flour
    milk
    bread
    sugar

Brown slices of pork and put aside. Pour off fat, reserving about two tablespoons. Mix fat and about four tablespoons flour. Over medium heat, gradually add milk, stirring to keep lumps from forming. Let come to a boil to thicken gravy. Serve gravy over a slice of bread. Sprinkle sugar over gravy. Serve with cooked pork slices.

Lamb in Cabbage
Får i kål

Mrs. Josefa Hansen Andersen of Chicago, Ill., writes, "I was born in Mandal, Norway, and came with my parents to the United States when I was a few months old. My parents owned the largest Norwegian restaurant in this country from 1915 to 1932 so I was raised in the food environment."

When Mrs. Andersen and her husband visited Norway several years ago they found it impossible to purchase lamb because Princess Astrid was entertaining friends on her yacht and had purchased all the local lamb in Fredrikstad. "Knowing the butcher, my husband was successful in obtaining lamb so we could have får i kål," Mrs. Hansen added. "Saint Hans Day, June 24th, is the longest day of the year and in Northern Norway the sun never sets. Får i kål is often served at gatherings on Saint Hans Day."

3 lbs. lamb stew meat, cut in 3-inch
cubes
1 cabbage, cut in 8 wedges
3 tsp. salt
1 Tbsp. whole peppercorns
¼ cup flour
¼ cup water

In a heavy pot, alternately layer cubes of lamb and wedges of cabbage. Sprinkle with salt. Place peppercorns in two cheesecloth bags and add to pot. Add water until it breaks to the surface of the top layer of meat. Simmer for 1½ hours or until meat is fork tender.

Remove bags of peppercorns and gently move layered stew to one side of the pot. Thicken stock with a mixture of flour and water. Gravy will be light in color since no frying has taken place. Rearrange stew into original position. Serve with boiled potatoes. Serves 5 or 6.

Lamb in Cabbage
Får i kål

This recipe comes from Birgitte Christianson of Decorah, Iowa, who was born in Copenhagen and whose husband teaches at Luther College and is assistant director for the academic affairs of the Norwegian-American Museum. "I am a real estate agent and am especially interested in historic preservation. I also do freelance translating from the Scandinavian languages into English.

"This is a traditional Norwegian dish, served both in the country and in the city in Norway. Many Norwegian-Americans are not aware of how much lamb and mutton are used in Norway. We have been served this old-fashioned and hearty dish in friends' homes there."

3 to 4 lbs. lamb, trimmed of all fat and
cut into 1½-inch cubes
3 Tbsp. butter or margarine
½ cup flour
3 cups chicken broth
1 large onion, sliced
2 lbs. white cabbage, coarsely sliced
2 Tbsp. salt, approximately
pepper to taste, about 2 tsp.

Brown lamb cubes in butter over medium heat a few at a time until evenly and nicely browned. Remove from pan as they are browned and place in a large bowl. Sprinkle meat with flour and toss until all pieces are well coated and all flour has disappeared. Pepper to taste.

In 6-quart ovenproof casserole layer lamb cubes, onion slices and cabbage slices, using half the ingredients each time. Salt each layer lightly. End with layer of cabbage.

Pour fat out of pan used to brown meat. Add chicken broth and boil, scraping browned meat residue from bottom of pan. Pour broth over meat and vegetables. Bake at 350 degrees F. 1½ to 2 hours or until meat is tender. Serves 6.

This is good with parsleyed boiled potatoes. It can be made ahead and reheated.

Cabbage Balls
Kål boller

Betty Nelson Seegmiller of Decorah, Iowa, is a former administrative assistant at Vesterheim.

1 15-oz. can sauerkraut
1 10¾-oz. can tomato soup
1 8-oz. pkg. lightly seasoned pork
    sausage
    regular rice
    cabbage leaves

Combine sauerkraut, tomato soup and one can water in heavy saucepan. (I prefer a large cast-iron kettle.) Bring to boil and simmer gently. Mix equal volumes of rice and pork sausage. Put 1 tablespoon mixture on cabbage leaf, roll up and secure with string or toothpicks. Place cabbage balls in pot with sauerkraut and tomato soup mixture and simmer gently for about four hours. Check occasionally to see that there is enough liquid so mixture will not burn. Serves 6-8.

"For ease in handling cabbage leaves, put the whole head in a small amount of boiling water and allow to cook just enough to peel off a leaf at a time without breaking it."

Norwegian Fish Balls
Fiskeboller

Violet D. Christophersen of Marinette, Wis., was one of the first three Rosemalers to win a Gold Medal. She writes: "Directions for this dish are given exactly the way it was taught to me many years ago. During the time-consuming process of preparing the fish balls, we dressed warm and worked in a cold room in order to keep the fresh fish from any possible spoilage."

2 quarts whole milk
2 dozen fresh herring or blue fins
4 small raw potatoes, peeled
1/3 cup soft butter, not melted
3 eggs, lightly beaten
¼ tsp. mace
¼ tsp. nutmeg
    salt and pepper to taste

Scald milk. Set aside to chill thoroughly. Scale fish, then clean. Remove the skin. Scrape off any meat adhering to the skin. Remove all bones.

Put all bones and skin into a kettle, add enough salted water to cover and let boil 10 minutes. Strain. Add enough water to the strained liquid to fill kettle half full. This liquid will be used to boil the fish balls in.

Grind the scraped fish through a meat grinder together with the peeled raw potatoes 3 to 5 times. Put well-ground fish into an extra large mixing bowl. With the help of a wooden potato masher, use a pounding and mashing effect on the ground fish until it forms tough dough. (An electric beater works well, too.) Add the soft butter and continue mashing. Add beaten eggs and the chilled milk, a cup at a time, with much pounding and mashing in between. Add the spices and seasoning to taste, being careful not to add too much spice. A delicate flavor is desired.

When the mass is light and fluffy, with a tablespoon first dipped in cold water then dipped into fish batter, drop like dumplings into the boiling fish broth. Let boil until done, about 7 or 8 minutes. The fish balls will rise to the surface when done.

Put fish balls into an earthen crock and pour the fish stock over all. It will keep for several weeks in a cold place. Or, you may pack some of the fish balls into sterilized jars, adding some of the liquid in which they were boiled. Seal jars and cook in hot water bath for one hour.

To serve, fry fish balls in butter until delicately browned.

Variation: make a boiled white sauce seasoned with salt and pepper and pour over fish balls.

Company Fish Balls in White Sauce
Selskaps fiskeboller i hvitsaus

Barbara Hamre Berg of Decorah, Iowa, studied weaving in Fagernes, Norway, at the Valdres Husflidskole. At Iowa State University she was in an Honors Program Project in Scandinavian Design. She is a freelance designer of both interiors and Scandinavian crafts. She says: "This dish was served to my husband and me when we visited cousins in Drammen, Norway. It was served over thin, shell-shaped pastries. A cucumber salad was also served."

1 14-oz. can fish balls
½ cup butter
½ cup flour
1 13-oz. can evaporated milk
fresh milk
1 6-oz. pkg. frozen shrimp, thawed, cooked and peeled
1 10-oz. pkg. frozen peas, thawed
¼ tsp. dill weed
salt and pepper to taste

Drain fish balls, reserving liquid. Quarter fish balls and set aside. Melt butter in saucepan, add flour and cook until well blended. Combine the fish liquid, evaporated milk and fresh milk to make 3 cups. Stir into butter-flour mixture and cook until smooth and hot.

Add the fish balls, shrimp and peas. Cook until heated through. Add the dill, salt and pepper. If too thick, add a little hot milk. Serve with puff pastry shells or with boiled potatoes. "There are never any leftovers."

"Uff Da"

"Uff da" is an expression widely used by Americans of Norwegian descent. It can be translated many ways, but "oh, dear" is close. *"Uff da"* is to a Norwegian what "Good grief" is to Charlie Brown. A joke in some Norwegian communities has it that *"uff da"* is being served Swedish meatballs at a *lutefisk* dinner.

Fish Balls in Curry
Fiskeboller i karrisaus

Eva Lund Haugen, who was born in Kongsvinger, Norway, sent this recipe. Her husband, Einar Haugen, is professor emeritus of Scandinavian and Linguistics at Harvard University. For 33 years he was chairman of Scandinavian studies at the University of Wisconsin. He is a member of the Board of Directors of the Norwegian-American Museum. Dr. Marion Nelson, museum director, suggested this fish ball recipe since he had enjoyed the dish in the Haugen home.

3 Tbsp. butter
3 Tbsp. flour
2 tsp. curry powder
½ cup fish stock, fish bouillon or chicken stock
1½ cups milk
1 16-oz. can Norwegian fish balls

Melt butter in a heavy-bottomed three-quart saucepan. Add flour and curry to melted butter. Stir for two minutes. Add stock and stir well. Add milk, stirring constantly. Simmer 10 minutes. Add fishballs and heat through on low heat. Serves three or four.

"If you wish to make it ahead, it can be reheated. It is normally served with boiled or steamed potatoes, green peas and carrots. Instead of fish balls, you can use cooked boneless and skinless fish. Instead of curry you could use 2 tablespoons drained capers which should be added before the simmering stage. This is a common everyday dish. We like a strong curry; you may want a bit less."

Sardines

Sardines caught in the summer are better than those caught in the winter. Called summer Brislings, they are usually packed in olive oil. Sild, or winter Brislings, are packed in soya oil or tomato or mustard sauce.

Lutefisk

Hyla Beroen Lehman of Cedar Rapids, Iowa, is a performing artist, lecturer and educator, "one hundred percent Norwegian by descent. Olaf Glosemodt, my father's great uncle, was a famed Norwegian sculptor in the 19th century, a contemporary of Ibsen and Grieg. In 1872 he carved from one solid block of marble the crowning chair used in the coronation of King Oscar in Christiania (later Oslo).

"On Christmas Eve lutefisk is traditionally served in our home with buttered lefse, boiled potatoes, cranberries or lingonberries and a green vegetable. Dessert features an elegant tray of assorted Christmas cookies, fruitcake and festive confections of all kinds. Coffee, of course!"

2 lbs. lutefisk
½ lb. butter, melted

Rinse fish thoroughly in cold water. Cut in pieces of serving size. Remove scales from any skin which you have not removed. If desired, tie fish in cheesecloth for cooking since it is very tender and will break apart. Place in cool salted water in four- or five-quart saucepan and bring to a boil. Cook for approximately 10 minutes or until tender and translucent. Remove gently and serve with generous amounts of melted butter. Serves four.

Cod Chowder
Torsk

Louise Fladager Sundet of Excelsior, Minn., writes: "My great grandfather, Mons Fladager, came to Spring Grove, Minn., from Valdres, Norway, in 1859. He purchased land and built a two-story frame building which became a general store. My father celebrated the 100th anniversary of the store, then in the family for three generations. Had I been born a boy, I would probably have been living in Spring Grove selling clothes in my father's store!" Mrs. Sundet is a board member of the Norwegian-American Museum.

1 cup chopped onion
¼ cup butter
4 cups diced raw potato
2 tsp. salt
½ tsp. coarsely ground black pepper
2 cups water
1 lb. frozen cod, partially thawed, cut in cubes
1 17-oz. can whole kernel corn, undrained
1 13-oz. can evaporated milk

In a large kettle, sauté onion in butter. Add potato, seasonings and water. Cover and simmer 15 minutes. Put cod on top of potatoes. Cover and simmer an additional 15 minutes. Stir in undrained corn and evaporated milk. Cover and heat to just below the boiling point.

"I sprinkle some parsley flakes on top to give it a little color!"

Poached Salmon
Kokt laks

Caron Gunnerud, St. Paul, Minn. This dish was served at the Nordic Brunch and Dinner fund-raiser for the Norwegian-American Museum in Decorah, Iowa.

1 gallon water
1 cup salt
2 lbs. fresh salmon, cut in slices
lemon wedges and parsley

Bring water and salt to boil. Add fish. Allow to simmer 12 to 15 minutes. Skim carefully to prevent gray film from forming on the fish. Serve salmon on a hot platter. Garnish with lemon wedges and parsley. Serves six.

Fish Soup
Fiskesuppe

Sigurd Daasvand of Oslo.

fish stock
2 carrots, sliced
1 parsnip, diced
1 stalk celery, sliced
green peas (optional)
1 heaping Tbsp. flour
1 cup top milk or cream
1 Tbsp. chopped chives or parsley
1 egg or ½ cup cream
½ tsp. vinegar and ½ tsp. sugar or
1 tsp. sweet relish (optional)

Use the skimmed stock obtained from boiling fish heads, skin and bones, when the rest of the fish is used for something else, or use the stock from canned fish balls, or use the water in which fish has been boiled the previous day. In this stock boil the sliced carrots, diced parsnip, celery and perhaps a few green peas.

When vegetables are tender, thicken soup with flour stirred with top milk or cream. After simmering for 10 minutes or more, add chopped chives or parsley.

Place egg, or a little cream, in the soup tureen and pour soup in while beating vigorously.

Some people like a little sour taste added to this soup. To obtain this flavor, a half teaspoon each of vinegar and sugar, a little sweet pickling syrup, or sweet relish may be added after removing soup from heat. But it is better that each person adds this to his or her taste, rather than to add it to the whole amount.

If fish balls are on hand, by all means add them to the soup after it has been thickened. Serve two or three in each soup plate. Diced potatoes and other vegetables may also be used.

Best

There is an old Norwegian saying, "If the fish is fresh, boiled is best."

Dumplings in Milk Soup
Melkesuppe med boller

Marion Nelson, director of the Norwegian-American Museum in Decorah, sends this recipe. It comes from his mother, Hilda Nelson of Fergus Falls, Minn., who was born in Aalesund in western Norway and emigrated to the United States from Lillehammer in 1903. She in turn got it from her mother, Maren Hagen Bergerson. Marion describes himself as "a farm boy from an immigrant family near Fergus Falls, Minn."

Soup:
1½ cups milk
1 tsp. sugar
¼ tsp. salt
Dumplings:
1 egg
½ tsp. sugar
⅛ tsp. salt
scant ⅛ tsp. nutmeg
1 tsp. vegetable oil
½ cup flour, approximately
1 Tbsp. butter or margarine

Combine soup ingredients in a 1½-quart saucepan (an enamel pan is good; a cast-iron enamel pan is even better). Heat to boiling.

While milk is heating prepare dumplings. Break egg into an ample-sized coffee cup, beating lightly with a fork. Add sugar, salt, nutmeg and oil. Add flour, beating until dough leaves the edge of the cup.

Using two teaspoons, pick up a ball of dough a scant teaspoonful in size and drop into slowly simmering milk. Lightly stir occasionally to prevent dumplings from settling to bottom. Simmer until dumplings have doubled in size, about five minutes. Add butter or margarine, allowing it to melt. Serve in soup bowls. Makes about 15 dumplings or two moderate servings.

"These dumplings are supposed to be quite firm. A salty meat such as dried beef is a good accompaniment."

Halvor Landsverk, Norwegian-American craftsman from Whalan, Minn., is a master woodcarver of *kubbestoler,* the chairs carved from single logs. These were in early farm homes throughout Norway. Landsverk selects and fells suitable basswood trees. After trimming the bark, he allows the wood to cure, and then does the final shaping and decorative carving. *Nordic Fest demonstration photograph by Darrell Henning.*

Potato Dumplings
Potet klubb

Doris Hagen Campbell of Rochester, Minn. She is a director of the National Bygdelag and Vesterheim.

- ½ **lb. salt pork**
- 6 **cups grated potatoes**
- 4 **cups flour**
- 2 **tsp. salt**

Cut salt pork into small cubes. Mix potatoes, flour and salt. Form this mixture into a 3 to 4 inch oval ball, placing a piece of salt pork in the center.

Place in boiling water and cook gently for 1½ hours.

"My family likes the *klubb* cooked with a ham, or if we can find corned beef without garlic, that also makes a flavorful dish.

"My grandmother from Sigdal taught my mother this family favorite. Now I have taught my daughters-in-law. When we fix *klubb,* I use a restaurant size soup kettle and triple the recipe.

"The next day I slice the *klubb* and fry it in butter. My family always makes sure there is enough *klubb* left over for this follow-up."

A *potet klubb* recipe was also sent to us from Dorothy Norby of Mabel, Minn., who writes, "My grandmother always served this on Christmas Eve and it is a 'must' in our family every year."

Norwegian Dumpling
Norsk klubb

Helen A. Falskerud Pilgrim of Decorah, Iowa. "This recipe was brought over from Norway by my mother."

- 1 **quart milk**
- 1 **Tbsp. salt**
- 1½ **cups graham or whole wheat flour**
- 3 **cups white flour**

In a large bowl put milk, salt and graham or whole wheat flour. Stir well and add white flour until mixture forms a large ball like bread dough.

Cut or pull off a piece of dough baseball size or larger and shape into a small loaf of bread. Heat a large kettle of water to boiling. Drop loaves into boiling water and boil for 1½ hours or until done when tested with a fork. An aluminum pie pan can be placed in bottom of kettle to keep *klubb* from sticking.

When done, take *klubb* out of kettle and cool. Slice in thin slices and fry in butter or margarine. Top with syrup. Or, instead of frying slices of *klubb,* half-and-half can be poured over slices.

"Good with fried bacon, ham, sausages or most any kind of meat. Makes about four loaves. They freeze well and can be reheated."

Above:

This is the traditional corner fireplace found in 19th century Norwegian homes. It is from Gudbrandsdal and is of carved soapstone. Corner fireplaces replaced fireplaces in the center of the room in medieval Norwegian dwellings. Cast iron stoves replaced the corner fireplaces. Kitchen utensils shown from left include a waffle iron, a circular hearth plate for baking *lefse* over coals, an iron kettle, sauce pan, round long handled *krumkake* iron, copper tea kettle and copper warming pan with birch handle. Vesterheim collection.

Opposite:

The Norwegian Folk Art Museum in Oslo, Norway, gave these costumed dolls by Norwegian doll-maker Rønnaug Petterssen to Vesterheim on its centennial in 1977. Norwegian designer Thorolf Holmboe designed the tapestry *The Animal Kingdom,* woven by Norwegian-American weaver Pauline Fjelde of Minneapolis, Minn., in the early 1900s. The candlestick was carved by Lars Fletre of Voss, Norway, in 1920. Fletre was active as a woodcarver and sculptor in Chicago for many years.

Lars Christenson of Benson, Minn., an immigrant, carved this 12′6″ by 10′3½″ altarpiece in 1897-1904. Christenson adapted realistic illustrations from an American-printed Norwegian Bible of the 1890s to his own primitive style. Discouraged by lack of interest in the congregation for whom the work was intended, Christenson never completed it. Like a true primitive, he spread the figures over the surface of the panels with sound decorative or symbolic principles but with little regard for spatial relationships. The overall plan follows a baroque type altar common in the parish churches of western Norway. After being exhibited at the 1904 Minnesota State Fair, the piece was stored until the death of the artist in 1910. It is displayed at the Norwegian-American Museum (Vesterheim) in Decorah, Iowa.

34

The Gudbrandsdal house at the Vesterheim museum has sparse simple Christmas decorations typical of those found in rural Norwegian homes over 100 years ago. White ceremonial towels cover windows, following an earlier holiday tradition still practiced in the Valdres district of Norway.

A straw mobile, a fertility symbol called an "unrest" or *uro*, hangs over the table. The artist who created it, the late William Jacobsen of Shell Rock, Iowa, had seen an *uro* from Norway in the historical museum in Copenhagen, when he was a little boy. He went home and tried to make one. His father, seeing him struggling with the craft, showed him the technique, which had been a common art when he was a child. One area of the *uro* represents the realm of the sun, another the moon. Vesterheim commissioned Jacobsen to make three examples for its collection. He used tiny squares of colored cloth cut with pinking shears to give accents to his crea-

tions. Sticks bound with straw form the structure.

This photograph of Lars and Mette Johnson of Decorah with their children Solveig and Lars-Erik at Vesterheim is available in a Christmas card from the Norwegian-American Museum. The card caption reads: "A bowl of beer and a large tub of butter dominated the Christmas table in rural Norway at the time of mass immigration a century ago. These are no longer symbols of Christmas to the Norwegian-American, but *rømmegrøt* (cream porridge) is still a favorite holiday dish. Finding an almond in it means good fortune. Reading the Christmas Gospel from the family Bible, originally kept in the corner cupboard behind father's seat, continues too. Tapestries, like the one of Herod's Feast in back of father, reminded early Norwegians that their feasting was a Christian ritual." *Photography by Bob Paulson, courtesy Don Padilla, Padilla and Speer, Inc., Minneapolis.*

The Westby Ship Gallery at Vesterheim displays a Norwegian vessel, the *Tradewind,* which sailed the Atlantic in 1933. Young sailor on the *Tradewind* is Erik David Wangsness Triebes, son of David and Linda Triebes of Des Moines, Iowa. Erik's *bunad* is of a style worn in western Norway's Sogn area from which his great, great, great great-grandfather came to America. A small tree is tied to the top mast of the ship every Christmas following a custom popular along the coastal areas of Norway and on Norwegian ships everywhere.

Viking ship float from Spring Grove, Minn. Iowan *Magazine photograph.*

Nordic Fest

Norwegian-Americans in Decorah, Iowa, say *"Velkommen"* to many guests year-round, but especially during the annual Nordic Fest the last full weekend in July, one of the most purely cultural festivals in the country.

At the Nordic Fest are demonstrations with pioneer equipment in spinning, carding, weaving, woodworking, metal working and blacksmithing. On display are major national exhibits of traditional Norwegian rosemaling, woodcarving and weaving as well as more local exhibits of hooked rugs, needlework, china painting and quilts. Traditional foods, dancing and music also abound.

Making goat cheese, Vesterheim.
Darrell Henning photograph.
Folk dancers, Decorah, Iowa.
Jack Anundsen photograph.

These two tankards in the Vesterheim collection represent two periods of the art of Herbjørn Sata, the man who founded the rosemaling tradition in Hallingdal. Dating from 1787 and 1804, they are choice documents of the origins of rosemaling in their area. The tankard at left was brought from Norway by an immigrant. The one on the right was a gift from a Norwegian museum.

Below: A display at Vesterheim contains these pieces of clothing, all decorated with free embroidery (as opposed to thread count embroidery like Hardanger). The cap and mittens at the lower right of the photograph are from Hallingdal. All the rest, the gloves, wool stocking, cotton cuff material and collar, are from Telemark.

Rosemaling at Vesterheim: Sigmund Aarseth from Volbu, Valdres, Norway, taught the first class in rosemaling at the Norwegian-American Museum. His panel, above left, incorporates an exciting variety of brushstrokes. Vi Thode of Stoughton, Wis., is represented with the vigorously patterned rosemaled trunk panel, above right. Ethel Kvalheim of Stoughton, Wis., uses subtle shades of colors to achieve a rich effect on the plate, below left. Gyda Mahlum of Beloit, Wis., painted the New Year's plate ("May fortune and progress follow you and yours in the new year"), below right. *Darrell Henning photographs.*

The rosemaling tree at Vesterheim is decorated in miniature wood cut-outs of objects which were part of Norwegian life: *kubbestoler,* animals, mittens, Christmas trees and others. Each has been decorated by award-winning rose-malers. Much of the contemporary rose-maling in the museum represents work by award winners in the annual national rosemaling exhibitions in Decorah.

Winners of the highest honor, the Gold Medal, come from Wisconsin, Michigan, Minnesota, Iowa and Washington states. They include: Gary Albrecht, Madison, Wis.; Violet Christophersen, Marinette, Wis.; Sallie DeReus, Leighton, Iowa; Carol Dziak, Greenfield, Wis.; John Gundersen, Minneapolis, Minn.; Barbara Hawes, Grand Rapids, Mich.; Karen Jenson, Milan, Minn.; Ethel Kvalheim, Stoughton, Wis.; Susan Louthain, Platteville, Wis.; Gyda Mahlum, Beloit, Wis.; Judith Nelson, Minneapolis, Minn.; Thelma and Elma Olsen, Elkhorn, Wis.; Dorothy Peterson, Ironwood, Minn.; Addie Pittelkow, St. Paul, Minn.; Eileen Riemer, Waukesha, Wis.; Agnes Rykken, Seattle, Wash.; Vi Thode, Stoughton, Wis.; Pat Virch, Marquette, Minn.; Trudy Wasson, Oelwein, Iowa; and Ruth Wolfgram, Franklin, Wis.

Above:

Surrounding the rosemaling tree is work by award winners in the Vesterheim collection. The cupboard in background was made by a Norwegian immigrant and painted by Martin Engseth of Minneapolis. It was part of a set of home furnishings belonging to Eleanor Hain of Minneapolis.

The Oneota Weavers Guild of Decorah made these decorations, left, using techniques traditional to Norway. The skirt was knit in a traditional block pattern by Mary Nentwick of Long Prairie, Minn., mother of Lila Nelson of the Vesterheim. Hanging in background is an åklæ (coverlet) of wool and linen from western Norway, a type woven by farm women throughout the country. Åklær were also used as decorative hangings on special occasions. The 8-pointed star motif is one of the oldest and most beloved of patterns.

Above:

Accomplished needleworker and teacher Grace Rikansrud of Decorah is wearing the festive costume of Amli, Aust-Agder, her ancestral home in southern Norway. The Vesterheim ornaments were created by friends of the museum. The items under the tree are worked in Klostersom and Hardanger by Grace. The carved table was given as a bequest by Mrs. Jorgine Slettede Boomer, who had it in her Waldorf-Astoria Hotel apartment in New York.

Christmas in immigrant homes in America is recreated in the Selland-Forde log house at Vesterheim. The tree is decorated with homemade heart-shaped paper baskets traditional in Norway. Some of these came from a Norwegian-American farmstead near Decorah and date from the turn of the century. Others are made by Birgitte Christianson of Decorah. The baskets held candy for the children.

The home of the Selland and Forde families was built of one large pine tree in 1852-53 in Big Canoe Township, 10 miles north of Decorah, Iowa. Legend has it that 17 people occupied this house during one winter in its early history.

The birch bookshelf dating from the late 1800s was made by John Johnson Forthun for the pioneer home of Thomas O. Forthun south of Viroqua, Wis. The shelf is of hand-planed boards and nailed construction, and has strong, primitive chip-carved decorations. The cradle is typical of immigrant cradles.

Opposite:

This Christmas tree with straw decorations is outside the Selland-Forde immigrant log house at Vesterheim. The decorations are by Maryanne Esgate of Decorah, Iowa, who demonstrates the craft regularly at the museum. Straw ornaments were traditional Norwegian decorations. In the background is a 1910 name or membership quilt. Embroidered in various blocks are the names of 20 pioneer members of the Highland Lutheran Church near Decorah.

Norma Wangsness of Decorah holds one of her costume dolls she painted of her own Telemark costume. Other provincial costumes represented are from Hallingdal, Voss, and Setesdal. She decorated the costume tree at Vesterheim. Norma's mother, Christina Lotvedt Anderson, stitched the embroidery on the red jacket when she was 85 years old. Six of the decorative buttons come from Norma's husband's great-grandmother's Telemark costume. The *soljer* (brooches) are heirlooms, too.

Rosettes, a traditional pastry, are popular at Christmas time in Norwegian homes.

Opposite:
Hilda Nelson of Fergus Falls, Minn., crocheted stars, baskets and pompons to adorn this tree at Vesterheim. The pompons of wool have a long tradition in Norwegian decoration. To the right on the table are the carders used to comb wool preparatory to spinning. The wheel is of a traditional type used for wool in Scandinavia. The objects in the case at left are examples of embroidery, appliqué and block printing on textiles from Norway.

The museum's program includes workshops in rosemaling, Norwegian embroidering and weaving, as well as wood carving and basketry.

At Christmas time the farmer set out a bowl of porridge (*grøt*) for the *nisse* to keep in his good graces, thereby helping to assure the well-being of the farm and its occupants. The little creatures (*nisser*) are prone to mischief. This one at Vesterheim, by Halvor Landsverk, Norwegian-American craftsman from Whalan, Minn., holds out a spider to scare the milkmaid.

The skis and sled were used by Norwegian immigrants.

The Norway building at Little Norway, with dragon heads at the peaks of the gables, was built in Trondheim, Norway. Peg construction allowed the building to be taken apart, shipped and reconstructed.

Above:

The sod roof at Little Norway is an example of the type of roof found on farm buildings or on a *seterhytte* (mountain hut) in Norway.

Little Norway
"Valley of the Elves"

Strolling through the grounds of Little Norway, 25 miles west of Madison, Wis., is like a mini-trip to the Norway of old combined with a trip back in time to American pioneer days.

Set in a deep valley are a dozen log houses that once were part of a pioneer homestead. In contrast is an ornate replica of a 12th Century *stavkirke* (Norwegian timber church) which is called the Norway Building. It was constructed for and sent to the Columbian Exposition of 1893 in Chicago. It was donated to Little Norway in 1935 by Phillip Wrigley. Contents include priceless antiques and memorbilia including a manuscript by Edvard Grieg, composer, and a piece of a Viking ship believed to be from the year 800.

The setting itself is like a slice of Norway—hills and valley and a winding stream. Osten Olson Haugen, a carpenter and stonemason from Tinn, Telemarken, Norway, settled here in 1856. His original dwelling is still standing.

The Haugen family farmed the valley more than 60 years. The buildings stood empty until 1926, when a Chicago insurance man, Isak Dahle, bought the property as a summer home.

He coined the name "Nissedahle" from the Norwegian *nissedal* (valley of the elves), altering the word to incorporate the family name. The buildings were furnished with antiques, some from Norway and others from pioneer America.

Little Norway was opened to the public shortly before Isak Dahle's death in 1937. His sister and her husband, Prof. and Mrs. Asher Hobson, then took over the management. Since then, over a million people have visited Little Norway.

Guides in colorful costumes conduct tours of the buildings, including a barn, granary, cobbler's shop, bachelor's cabin, spring house and sod-roofed cottage. The season is May 1 through the last Sunday in October. There is an admission charge.

The guides and staff of Little Norway are shown with antiques including, left, Jane Hobson, holding a Hardanger 8-string violin, and Mildred Thronson, sitting in an antique 6-legged rocker, both wearing national costumes from Valdres, Elaine Reilly, in a Hardanger costume, and Emma Lund, standing behind a pioneer spinning wheel, wearing a West Telemark costume. Oljanna Cunneen, wearing a costume from Lom, Gudbrandsdal, is holding a Norwegian *lur*, the kind of horn sounded by the young Norwegian girl Prillar-Guri to warn the people of marauding Scots in the 17th century. Ethelyn Thompson is wearing the Valdres costume from Øystre Slidre,

Marsellia Hagan is in Hardanger costume and Marcelaine Winner is in the costume of Lillehammer, Gudbrandsdal.

Antiques in the photograph include two rosemaled chairs (the black and tan ones) by Per Lysne of Stoughton, Wis., who started the rosemaling revival in America, and a round trunk dated 1836, once owned by Kari Hansdatter. Girls stored lace handiwork in round hope chests, carrying them up the mountains when they herded cattle in the summers. The small container on the ground near the antique spinning wheel is a ship's water ration for one day for an immigrant passenger. An 1834 ale bowl is also shown.

The *stabbur* is built on a raised foundation. On Norwegian farms such a design protects stored food. The wood carvings of this *stabbur* are by Olin Ruste who worked at Little Norway. At left is the original farm home built by the Norwegian immigrant Haugen family. Nearby is the dugout where they spent their first winter in the valley in 1856.

Marilyn Wang Engwall of Rochester, Minn., wears a costume made for her at the Husflid in Elverum, Norway. This *bunad* represents the Østerdal Valley, the easternmost part of the Hedmark district. Her handmade costume is woven of wool. The vest is a damask brocade. The shirt is linen with white embroidery on cuffs, collar and shoulders. Jewelry is sterling silver. Marilyn's hat of silk brocade comes from France and this style is worn only by married women.

The objects are in a built-in cupboard in the replica of a Telemark farmhouse on the first floor of Vesterheim. The top shelf holds a milk container of stave construction, a carved ale bowl, another stave-constructed milk bucket and a covered lunch box of bentwood construction. The second shelf holds a coffee grinder and a milk strainer. The earliest coffee grinders took the form of mortars and pestles; these box types with a metal grinding mechanism were a later development.

The lower shelf shows a milk strainer resting on a milk container of stave construction. The strainers held filters of hair from cows' tails worked in a looped technique called knotless netting through which milk was poured. A cheese press is beside the milk container. In the back is a footed wood pedestal plate holding bread. Marilyn holds a low footed plate with a block of molded butter.

53

Mike and Else Sevig, folksingers from Minneapolis, Minn., and their daughter Mari are shown with Else's Christmas baking. In the foreground is *kringle.* At the top of the tray are *serinakaker,* and from left to right are *sandbakkels, rosetter,* *sprutbakkels, sandbakkels* filled with strawberries and whipping cream, *lefse* and *kransekake.* Mike's costume is from Rogaland and Else's is from Vest-Agder. Mari's costume is from Gudbrandsdal. *Photograph by John Louis Anderson.*

Ida Askelson Sacquitne of Decorah demonstrated *lefse*-making at the Smithsonian Institution in Washington, D.C., during the nation's 1976 Bicentennial. The traditional Norwegian breads were rolled out with grooved rolling pins and baked on round iron plates over an open fire. The flatbreads, thin and crisp, were made from rye flour and milk or water, while *lefse,* which is generally thicker and often soft, may include potatoes which are mashed or ground in a wood grinder. Both types of bread kept well in clean mountain air and were stacked in storehouses. From there they were carried to the dwelling in large round baskets woven from fine birch roots.

Marilyn Skaugstad of Iowa City, Iowa, baked these Christmas foods for her family. Clockwise, from the top the foods include *haring kake* and spiced hermits. The tray holds rosettes, *spritz, kringle,* potato cakes, *sandbakkels* and *krumkake. Julekake* is the Norwegian Tea Ring. Fruit soup is in the compote. The antique rosemaled wooden bowl contains nuts.

The antique tablecloth was made by Marilyn's grandmother Torbjorg Gunnerson-Sekse Olson, who brought it to America in the early 1900s. It is a Scandinavian embroidery called Hardanger. The delicate silver spoons are from her family in Norway.

"All the recipes are family favorites from my mother and her mother, Torbjorg," said Marilyn. "A snack we had at Grandma's was called *skjebrød,* a slice of homemade bread served with milk and sugar. My children still enjoy it and call it by name with special affection for Grandma."

Overleaf:

Arla Erickson Lyon of Decorah, Iowa, bakes *kransekake* professionally. Her maternal grandparents came from Sunnfjord, Norway, and her paternal grandfather came from Christiania, Norway, in 1854. The Vesterheim cupboard in the background is a reproduction of one used in Gudbrandsdal during the 19th century, a type generally placed near the door to contain pans of milk. The farmers allowed milk to sour, and it was eaten as a pudding or stirred into water for a drink. The *åklæ* (coverlet) is one using a traditional Norwegian tapestry technique. This example has the eight-petal flower of the type made in Sogn and dates from the late 18th century.

Salads and More

In Norway, salads did not develop as part of the national cuisine. The ingredients just weren't available, according to Marion Nelson, director of Vesterheim. "Carrots and cabbage are served around meat dishes rather than as a separate dish," he said.

Pickled Beets
Rødbeter

Mary Holum of Minneapolis provided the hotel chef with her recipe for pickled beets for the 1980 Nordic Brunch and Nordic Dinner in Minneapolis. Sponsored by Twin Cities Friends of the Norwegian-American Museum, more than 1,000 people eager to learn more about their heritage attend the annual festivities.

- ½ cup white vinegar
- ½ cup sugar
- 1 1-lb. can sliced beets, including juice
- ½ to 1 tsp. salt
- pepper to taste
- whole cloves, optional

In a stainless steel or enameled 1½- to 2-quart saucepan combine vinegar, sugar, juice from beets, salt and pepper. A few whole cloves tied in a cloth bag can be added, if desired. Bring to a boil and boil briskly for two minutes.

Meanwhile, place sliced beets in a deep glass, stainless steel or enamel bowl. Pour hot marinade over beets and let them cool, uncovered. When mixture reaches room temperature, cover bowl with plastic wrap and refrigerate at least 12 hours.

He Coined a Phrase

In 1899, economist Thorsten Veblen, who was of Norwegian descent, wrote *Theory of the Leisure Class,* a book which gave birth to the term "conspicuous consumption."

Sweet-Sour Cabbage
Surkål

Josefa Hansen Andersen of Chicago

- 1 head cabbage
- 1 tsp. salt
- 2 Tbsp. sugar
- ¼ cup vinegar
- 2 Tbsp. caraway seed

Shred cabbage very fine. Add other ingredients. Cover with water and simmer for 2 to 3 hours. Good served with roast pork.

Cranberry Salad

Adella Askvig Valen, wife of the Rev. Elmer Valen, who serves as visitation pastor on the staff of First Lutheran Church in Decorah, Iowa, sent this recipe.

"This recipe should serve seven or eight people. It is a very simple salad and can be made ahead of time. It is very good with a turkey or chicken dinner and has always been a favorite of our children at Thanksgiving and Christmas. When unable to come home, they have been known to telephone from faraway places to check on ingredients and method of preparation."

- 3 cups thick cranberry sauce
- 2/3 cup graham cracker crumbs
- ½ pint whipping cream, whipped sugar
- ½ tsp. vanilla

Make cranberry sauce with your usual recipe, perhaps using a little less water to make it thicker. Save a few whole cranberries for garnish.

Sweeten whipped cream to taste and add vanilla. Layer cranberry sauce, crumbs and whipped cream in a clear glass bowl, repeating in same order.

Herring Pâté
Sildepâté

Ruth Wickney, Northwood, N.D.

1 12-oz. jar herring in cream or wine
   sauce, drained
1 8-oz. pkg. cream cheese
½ cup pitted ripe olives
1/3 cup chopped parsley
¼ to ½ tsp. curry powder
   juice of half a lemon

Place all ingredients in blender and process at highest speed until smooth. Place mixture in a crock and chill.

Excellent on party rye with chopped olives and hard-cooked egg garnish. It can also be used with raw vegetables.

Cranberry Catsup
Tyttebœr ketchup

Esther M. Johnson, Ossian, Iowa.

1 lb. cranberries
½ cup mild vinegar
2/3 cup water
1 cup brown sugar
½ tsp. cloves
½ tsp. ginger
½ tsp. paprika
1 tsp. cinnamon
½ tsp. salt
¼ tsp. pepper
2 Tbsp. butter

Put cranberries, vinegar and water in pan and boil until berries are soft (about five minutes). Put through food mill. Add the brown sugar, spices and seasoning and simmer three minutes. Add the butter. Serve at room temperature.

"Cranberry catsup can be refrigerated for months. It's great on roast pork or turkey."

Reminiscences

Hilda Nelson of Fergus Falls, Minn., who was born in Norway, reminisced for us about cooking on the family farm in Swan Lake Parish, Ottertail County, Minnesota, in the 1920s and 1930s.

Recipes didn't really mean much in the Depression. It was a matter of making anything reach as far as possible.

I creamed many things because it made them good and they went much further: for example, peas, tuna or salmon, and potatoes.

If plenty of cooked potatoes were left from dinner, a little meat with onion could be stretched to make a good hash. When this went through the meat grinder, a slice of dry bread was ground last to be sure that no bit of meat remained to go to waste in the grinder.

Even leftover pancakes were not wasted. They were cut in squares the next morning and simmered a bit in rich milk. This was served in soup plates with a sprinkle of sugar for breakfast.

Dessert for dinner was often a bit of leftover fruit sauce of any kind or a pint jar of juice from any fruit or berry, which was thickened with cornstarch and served, of course, with a bit of cream over it.

Salt herring, another standby, was cleaned and then simmered a little in water, drained and simmered next in rich milk or cream. This made wonderful gravy for the potatoes.

Prunes and raisins were the base for sweet soup. I added any bits of fruit and sauce I had. A stick of cinnamon was a must. Wild grape juice made it special. My mother in Norway used lingonberries, but I never had them here. Sometimes I added macaroni to give a richer and thicker soup. It did not change the taste and it increased the amount.

When the church choir practiced, I made them sponge cake with a custard sauce on it. We had the eggs and milk on the farm, so there was nothing to buy.

Breads

Hardanger Lefse
Haringkake

Marilyn Skaugstad of Iowa City, Iowa.

3 pkgs. dry yeast
1 cup warm potato water
6 cups milk, scalded
1 cup sugar
¾ cup vegetable shortening or lard
1 Tbsp. salt
4 cups graham flour
9 to 10 cups all-purpose flour

Soften yeast in warm potato water 5 to 10 minutes. To scalded milk add sugar, shortening and salt. Let cool. Combine yeast with milk and add graham flour. Beat mixture until smooth. Let set until it makes soft sponge, about 1 hour. Add enough flour to make soft dough. Put dough in greased bowl; turn over to grease surface. Cover and let rise in warm place until double.

Shape into small buns about the size of an egg and let rise on greased sheets. Roll out thinly, first using lefse rolling pin and then using the special *Haringkake* rolling pin. Use plenty of flour to keep dough from sticking to board. Fold over clean stick and transfer sheet of dough to electric *lefse* plate and bake at low setting until browned on both sides. Put on clean towel to cool and become crisp. Will keep indefinitely if stored in a dry place.

Before serving, dip each sheet of *Haringkake* in cold water, drain and wrap in towel or wax paper to soften. Spread sheets with butter and any variety of assorted toppings; sugar, jams, cheeses, cold meats or peanut butter. Roll up and cut to size as desired.

West Coast Lefse
Kraatekake

Olive Nordby of Madison, Wis., writes: "This was Dr. (Eugene) Nordby's mother's recipe (Lucile Korsrud Nordby). We all liked Kraatekake *better than* lefse. *I would help her, as it's easiest with two working, taking turns rolling and frying. Even then, the dough fights back and it's difficult." Dr. Nordby has been president of the board of the Norwegian-American Museum in Decorah since 1968. All four of his grandparents came from Norway in the 1860s to the Decorah, Ia., and Lee, Ill., areas. Olive's parents were from the Drammen area of Norway.*

2 pkgs. yeast
4 cups milk
½ cup butter
½ cup sugar
12 to 14 cups flour

Mix as for bread; dough should be a little firmer than bread. Let rise. Knead down, let rise again until light. Divide into good-sized biscuits and cover with damp cloth to keep from drying out. Roll each one out on floured cloth with grooved rolling pin until thin, as for lefse. This is difficult as dough springs back. Use sharp pointed rolling pin to mark. Bake on hot greased griddle, turning as one side browns. Spread out cakes until cool and crisp. Makes about 50.

To serve, place between dampened dish towels until softened to consistency of *lefse*. Spread with butter and sugar as you would *lefse*.

"I make half a recipe, about 28 cakes. These can be stored in covered containers or plastic sacks indefinitely when dry."

Lefse rolling pins, Vesterheim.

Lefse
Lefse

Ida Sacquitne of Decorah, Iowa, demonstrated lefse-making at the Norwegian-American Museum in Decorah and annually for the Nordic Fest. Her father came to Decorah with his parents at age 8 from Voss. "Hard times in Norway caused them to make the move."

5 well-packed cups riced potatoes
½ cup margarine
3 Tbsp. powdered sugar
2 cups flour
1 tsp. salt

Use Idaho russet potatoes. Boil, then mash and rice potatoes. Add margarine while potatoes are still warm. Cool until room temperature. Add powdered sugar, flour and salt. Mix with your hands. Knead well and then roll into a log.

Cut and measure into 1/3-cup portions and make a round ball of each portion. Press it down by hand and it will be easier to keep round while rolling out.

Dust the large canvas-like cloth *lefse* "board" with flour. Press dough down, turn over and press down again. Roll as thin as possible with a rolling pin with a pastry sleeve into large 14-inch circles to fit *lefse* grill. The secret of making *thin lefse* is using a covered rolling pin. The last roll across dough use grooved *lefse* rolling pin, which marks the dough slightly and makes it thinner.

Use a *lefse* stick and roll dough on stick and transfer to *lefse* grill. You must use a *lefse* stick or holes will be made in the dough. Bake on hot *lefse* grill or a griddle. Bake a minute or two, then turn with a *lefse* stick. Turn when bubbles and brown spots appear. Fold each *lefse* in half or quarters. Cool between towels and store in plastic bag. Makes about 18.

Spread with butter to eat. Some people sprinkle brown or white sugar on it. Roll up.

Mother's Dark Rye Bread
Mors rugbrød

Florence Shjeflo Buck of Tacoma, Wash., is a member of the board of the Norwegian-American Museum in Decorah, Iowa, and a member of the Collegium and Scandinavian Cultural Council at Pacific Lutheran University. She teaches rosemaling and was co-founder of the Western Rosemalers Association of which she is a past president. Her father came from Trondheim, and her mother's family from Østfold.

"This bread was always baked by my mother, Judith Nellie Rudd Shjeflo of North Dakota, when any of the children returned home after a lengthy absence. The aroma of fresh homemade bread, butter and her special homemade jam served with coffee was the sweetest welcome we ever wanted."

1 cup warm water
2 Tbsp. sugar
2 pkg. dry yeast
2 cups white flour
1½ cups dark rye flour
1 tsp. salt
½ cup plus 1 Tbsp. molasses
1¼ cups hot water
2 Tbsp. melted shortening
4 cups white flour, approximately

In small mixing bowl add sugar to warm water. Dissolve. Sprinkle yeast over water. Set aside.

Put 2 cups white flour and the dark rye flour in large mixing bowl. Add salt and mix. Add molasses thinned with hot water. Add melted shortening. Mix. Add yeast. Mix. Gradually add remaining flour. Flour bread board and knead dough 8 to 10 minutes, until elastic. Put dough in greased bowl and let rise until double in bulk.

Punch down and knead lightly. Divide into 3 equal portions. Shape into loaves and place in three individual 9 x 5 greased glass loaf pans. Let rise. When double in size, bake in preheated oven at 375 degrees F. for approximately 50 minutes.

Whole Wheat Bread
Hvetebrød

Dagny A. Schiotz of Minneapolis was the daughter of the Rev. A.O. Aasen, who emigrated from Norway and was a pastor of the Lutheran church until his death at 100 years of age. Her husband, the Rev. Fredrik A. Schiotz, has an illustrious background in the Lutheran church. He has served as president of the American Lutheran church and of the Lutheran World Federation of 70 million members. He is on the board of directors of the Norwegian-American Museum in Decorah. His autobiography, One Man's Story, *was published by the Augsburg Publishing House. The Rev. Mr. Schiotz says of this recipe: "There has been one item in her baking that I have especially enjoyed. I refer to her whole wheat bread. Many people have tasted it and given it solid approval."*

    1 tsp. sugar
    3 pkgs. dry yeast
    ½ cup lukewarm potato water
    1 Tbsp. apple cider vinegar
    1¾ cups warm milk
    ½ cup oil (sunflower or sesame, if you
        wish)
    ½ cup dark molasses
    ½ cup brown sugar, firmly packed
    ½ cup rolled oats
    1 egg, beaten
    1 Tbsp. honey
    1 cup whole wheat flour (or ½ cup soy
        flour and ½ cup rice flour)
    1 cup rye flour
    5 cups white flour
    1 tsp. salt
        sesame seed

Dissolve sugar and yeast in potato water. Set aside.

In large bowl, combine vinegar (to retard mold), milk, oil, molasses, brown sugar and oats. Stir thoroughly. Add yeast mixture, beaten egg and honey. Add flours and salt and beat vigorously until smooth.

Turn out on floured board. Add more flour as needed. Knead until elastic, about ½ hour. Put into greased bowl; turn once or twice. Cover. Wrap bowl in plastic bag. Let rise until double.

Divide into three parts. Shape into loaves. Dip loaves into milk, then into sesame seed. Place in greased pans, cover and let rise until double in size.

Bake at 350 degrees F. about 45 to 50 minutes. To test, tap crust for hollow sound. Remove from pans and cover to cool.

Oatmeal Flatbread
Havremel flatbrød

Norma Anderson Wangsness of Decorah is a rosemaler and a photographic craftsman.

    ½ cup sugar
    ¾ cup melted butter
    ½ tsp. salt
    1½ cups buttermilk
    1 tsp. soda
    3 cups white flour (or 2 cups white
        and 1 cup whole wheat)
    2 cups quick-cooking oats

Cream together sugar and melted butter. Add salt. Add soda to buttermilk and then add to the creamed mixture alternately with the flour. Add the oats.

Divide mixture into 2 log shapes. Divide, as you work, into 1/3-cup portions and shape each into a round ball. Press down and roll on pastry cloth with a rolling pin covered with pastry sleeve. Roll until paper-thin. Use a *lefse* stick and roll the dough on stick; lift and unroll on cookie sheet.

Either cut with pastry cutter into squares before baking or bake and then break into pieces. Bake at 350 degrees F. until lightly browned, about 8 minutes. Remove and stack. Store in covered container.

"We like to spread it with butter. You may use pickled herring with it or *gjetost* (goat cheese). It can also be served on an hors d'oeuvre tray."

Coffee Braid
Kaffe kranz

Sylvia Rusley Simonson of Minneapolis, whose husband is now a member of the board of directors of the Norwegian-American Museum at Decorah, Iowa, writes: "For 31 years I was a pastor's wife and for four years the wife of the U.S. ambassador to Ethiopia, so entertaining was a necessity."

2 cups milk, scalded
1 cup butter
2 pkgs. dry yeast
¼ cup lukewarm water
1 tsp. sugar
5 eggs, well beaten
1¼ cups sugar
1 tsp. vanilla
1 to 2 tsp. cardamom
7¾ cups unbleached flour
Frosting:
1 egg, beaten
½ cup butter
1 pound powdered sugar
½ tsp. vanilla
½ tsp. almond flavoring
chopped nuts for topping

Scald milk, add butter and let cool until lukewarm. Dissolve yeast in lukewarm water with 1 teaspoon sugar. Beat eggs well; add 1¼ cups sugar and beat. Pound cardamom in a pestle until fine. Add vanilla and cardamom to mixture. Add flour and beat well. Let rise until double in bulk.

Put on floured board, adding more flour (as little as possible) before dividing into three parts. Roll out one at a time in rectangular shape, about 10 X 14 inches. Cut lengthwise into six strips, braiding by threes to make six braids in all. Put two braids on each cookie sheet. Let rise about two hours in cold oven out of drafts.

After removing dough, preheat oven to 350 degrees F. Bake 15 minutes. When cool, frost with frosting made by beating egg with butter, powdered sugar and flavorings. Sprinkle nuts on top.

Christmas Bread
Julekake

Barbara Hanson Bulman, Forest City, Iowa. "Both of my grandfathers were John Hansons from Norway. My paternal grandfather was from Telemark and was known as John K. Hanson. My maternal grandfather was from Gudbrandsdal, and he was known simply as John Hanson. My brother John K. Hanson carries on the family name. All four of my grandparents came from Norway via sailship after long difficult journeys."

½ cup butter or margarine
2 cups sugar
3 eggs
5 cups flour
2 tsp. baking powder
2 cups heavy sour cream
1 tsp. soda dissolved in small
    amount of warm water
1 tsp. ground cardamom

Cream butter or margarine and sugar. Add eggs. Add sifted dry ingredients with sour cream and soda.

Divide dough in three parts and put in bread loaf pans. Bake for 45 minutes at 350 degrees F., or until it pulls away from sides of pans. Cakes should be golden.

While still hot, slice quickly and carefully as you would bread. It is rich and crumbles easily. Place slices on cookie sheets and toast in oven until lightly browned and dry, but not too brown.

After it is cooled, store in flat container to keep from crumbling, as it is dry.

"Our family wants it especially for holidays and visits home. You have to taste it to love it. Such a fun one to dunk!"

Nobel Peace Prize

Dr. Norman E. Borlaug, an agriculturist, won the 1970 Nobel Peace Prize for his efforts in developing high-yielding strains of wheat that are resistant to disease. Born in Cresco, Iowa, he received a Ph.D. degree in plant pathology from the University of Minnesota in 1941.

Christmas Bread
Julekake

Trudy Sondrol Wasson of Oelwein, Ia., is a professional rosemaler. She was awarded the Medal of Honor in Rosemaling from Vesterheim in 1976. She teaches in several states as well as at Vesterheim. "My dad is from Valdres and my mother's parents are from eastern Norway. I have been to Norway twice to research old rosemaling."

2 cakes yeast
½ cup lukewarm water
3 cups milk, scalded
½ cup butter
¾ cup sugar
10 cups flour, sifted
2 tsp. salt
2 eggs
½ cup currants
½ cup chopped citron
¾ cup chopped raisins
½ cup candied cherries
½ tsp. cardamom
   egg white for glaze
   butter for brushing
   cinnamon/sugar mixture for
     sprinkling

Dissolve yeast in lukewarm water. Pour scalded milk over butter. When cooled to lukewarm, add yeast and sugar. Add half of flour and salt and beat well for 10 minutes. Add eggs, one at a time, and beat thoroughly. Add fruit, cardamom and remaining flour. Knead and place in greased bowl to rise. Cover and set in warm place. When dough has doubled in bulk, knead again. Let rise until light.

Shape into loaves and place in greased pans. Brush tops of loaves with egg white. When doubled in bulk, bake at 350 degrees F. for 35 to 40 minutes. After removing from oven, brush crusts with melted butter and sprinkle with cinnamon and sugar.

"Makes four loaves. You can use either pie pans or loaf pans. Freezes well. I usually triple the recipe and make a dozen loaves. One or two usually get eaten as soon as they are baked."

Norwegian Christmas Bread
Julekake

Eunice C. Stoen of Decorah has published her own cookbook called "Euny's Cookbook." She and her husband Wilbur live on a dairy and hog farm in northeast Iowa.

2 pkgs. dry yeast
½ cup warm water
1 tsp. sugar
1 cup milk, scalded
½ cup butter
1 egg, beaten
½ cup sugar
½ tsp. salt
¾ tsp. cardamom
5 cups flour, approximately
½ cup citron
½ cup candied cherries
½ cup white raisins

Dissolve yeast in warm water and a little sugar. Scald milk and add butter; cool to lukewarm. Add egg and then yeast mixture. Add sugar, salt and cardamom. Beat in 2 cups flour and mix well. Mix fruit with a little of the remaining flour so it doesn't stick together and add. Stir in rest of flour.

Knead on floured cloth until smooth. Place in greased bowl. Cover and let rise until doubled. Divide into two parts and form round loaves. Put on greased cookie sheets or pie pans. Let rise until nearly double.

Bake at 350 degrees F. for 30 to 40 minutes. While warm brush with soft butter or decorate with powdered sugar icing mixed with almond flavoring, then almonds and more candied cherries.

"This is a Christmas bread, but I use it other times, too. Slice a round loaf, cut slices in half on an angle or in smaller pieces, butter and serve as fancy sandwiches. This is delicious toasted, buttered and served with tea. It makes a pretty gift, wrapped in foil with a big red bow on top."

This ale bowl in the Vesterheim collection came to the Norwegian-American Museum from an immigrant family in Dawson, Minn. It is typical of a type found in Voss in western Norway and other areas. The ale bowl with horsehead handles has a prototype in dragon-headed ale bowls of the Middle Ages. The form is near that of the Viking ships, and the name for an early type, *kane*, is the same as for a small boat.

Christmas Bread
Julebrød

Martha Torrison of Schaumburg, Ill., a member of the board of directors of the Norwegian-American Museum at Decorah, Iowa. "My grandparents came from Norway. After several moves they ended up in Manitowoc, Wis., where they raised a family of 10 sons and two daughters. My father, one of the twelve, became a doctor."

- 2 cups milk, scalded
- 1 or 2 cakes yeast
- ¼ cup warm water and 1 Tbsp. sugar
- 1 cup sugar
- 7 to 8 cups flour
- ½ cup butter
- 1 cup raisins
- 1 cup cut-up citron
- 2 tsp. cardamom
- ½ cup blanched almonds
- 2 tsp. salt

Scald milk and cool to lukewarm. Dissolve yeast in warm water and 1 Tbsp. sugar. To the milk add sugar, yeast and half of the flour. Beat thoroughly. Add butter, fruit, cardamom, nuts, salt and enough flour to make a stiff dough. Knead, cover and let rise until double.

Form two loaves. Let rise. When double in bulk, bake at 350 degrees F. about 1 hour.

Bishop's Bread
Brød

Ruth Wickney of Northwood, N.D., is on the board of directors of the Norwegian-American Museum in Decorah. She says this recipe is "elegant for the holidays and especially for those who do not like fruitcake. It freezes well. This was Mrs. J.A. Aasgard's recipe. Dr. Aasgard was the presiding bishop of the Norwegian Lutheran Church before the days of current mergers."

- 1 cup sugar
- 3 eggs
- 1½ cups flour
- 1½ tsp. baking powder
- 1 cup whole walnuts
- 1 cup whole Brazil nuts
- 1 cup whole maraschino cherries
- 1 cup whole pitted dates
- 1 8-oz. bar semi-sweet or sweet chocolate, cut in large chunks

Mix sugar and eggs well. Add flour and baking powder. Mix well. Add whole nuts, cherries, dates and chocolate. Hand mix. Prepare loaf pan by lining with heavy waxed paper. Pour batter into lined pan. Cover pan loosely with excess waxed paper. Bake at 325 degrees F. 1 hour and 25 minutes. Fold back the waxed paper when batter has risen (about 50 to 60 minutes after it has been in oven).

Oatmeal Crackers
Havrekjeks

Jackie Bjoin of Golden Valley, Minn. first tasted these crackers at Skogfjorden, the Norwegian Language Camp, and then made them to serve to the kick-off committee for the Nordic Brunch in Minneapolis. They are delicious and easy to make.

1 cup cornflakes
1 cup bran flakes
2 cups rolled oats
2 cups flour
½ cup sugar
1 cup margarine
1 tsp. soda
½ cup hot water

Measure cornflakes and bran flakes and then crush. Add oats, flour and sugar. Cut in margarine with pastry blender. Add soda which has been dissolved in hot water. Blend well. Divide dough into four equal parts. With a sleeve-covered *lefse* rolling pin, roll out each part separately to 1/16th-inch thick on a floured pastry cloth. With a pizza or *fattigmann* cutter, cut into 2" X 3" rectangles. Place on an ungreased cookie sheet. Bake for 8 to 10 minutes at 350 degrees F. Cool. Crackers are tender, so store carefully.

Hardtack

Dagney Johansen is a student at the Scandinavian Language Institute and we received her recipe from Issa Parker of the Nordic Heritage Museum in Seattle, Washington. Director Marion Nelson of Vesterheim says the Norwegian breakfast often includes hardtack, a rye bread and a thin crisp flatbrød.

2 cups white flour
2 cups graham flour
½ cup white sugar
1 tsp. soda
½ tsp. salt
1 Tbsp. anise seed
½ cup shortening
1½ cups buttermilk

Mix dry ingredients. Cut in shortening. Add buttermilk. Roll out thinly. Cut into diamond-shaped pieces. Place on a greased cookie sheet. Bake at 400 degrees F. for 12 to 15 minutes.

Rusks
Kavring

Thora Leonard of Story City, Iowa: "I have had the good fortune to visit the Scandinavian countries. From pleasant memories of my visit I say, 'Jeg kan ikke glemme gamle Norge!'"

½ cup margarine
1/3 cup sugar
1 cup white flour
1 cup whole wheat or rye flour
1 tsp. soda
2 tsp. baking powder
½ tsp. cream of tartar
¾ cup buttermilk

Cream together margarine and sugar. Sift together other dry ingredients. Add to creamed mixture alternately with buttermilk. Roll flat with rolling pin to ¼-inch thickness on lightly floured pastry board. Cut 2-inch rounds. Place on ungreased baking sheet and bake at 400 degrees F. until light brown.

Split each biscuit in half. Place on baking sheet and bake at 200 degrees about five minutes or until light brown. Makes about 4 dozen. Can be frozen.

"These *kavrings* are made especially for Christmas festivities in Norwegian homes. We always serve them for breakfast Christmas Day."

The Holland Tunnel

It was a Norwegian, Ole Singstad, who conceived the idea for the Holland Tunnel below the Hudson River in New York. It was the first tunnel large enough to permit automotive traffic. Singstad was considered the world's leading authority on tunnels.

Cakes

Blitz Torte

Marlys Lien of Calmar, Iowa, received this recipe from her mother-in-law, Grace Lien. Grace's mother Cecilia Borness also enjoyed this cake. "Engvold Borness, Cecilia's husband, came to America in 1902 at the age of 21. He began working on farms, earning about $25 a month in the summer. In the winter he worked in lumber camps. So many grandchildren and great-grandchildren loved him and enjoyed his tales of coming to America. I feel so fortunate to have known Engvold and Cecilia."

    4 egg yolks
    ½ cup butter
    ½ cup sugar
      scant 1 cup flour
    5 Tbsp. milk
    1 tsp. vanilla
      dash salt
    1½ tsp. baking powder
Meringue:
    4 egg whites
    ¾ cup sugar
      nuts
Filling:
      pudding or whipped cream

Beat egg yolks, butter and sugar. Add flour, milk, vanilla, salt and baking powder. Beat well. Put in two layer pans, which have been greased and lined with foil. Beat 4 egg whites until stiff. Add ¾ cup sugar slowly, mixing well. Spread this meringue mixture on cakes before baking. Sprinkle with nuts. Bake at 350 degrees F. for 20 minutes. Lift out onto wax paper to cool. Place one cake on serving plate, meringue side down. Put filling of pudding or whipped cream on top of meringue. Place other layer on top, meringue side up.

"This has been the most asked for birthday cake in our family for many years. It has become a birthday tradition."

Great-grandmother's Gingerbread
Oldemors pepperbrød

Norma Wangsness of Decorah sends this recipe, which was a favorite of her mother, Christina Lotvedt Anderson. "She lived to be 90," writes Norma, "and she started the embroidery of my costume (bunad) when she was 80, finishing when she was 85. She did better embroidery at 80 than she did at 60.

"This recipe is over 100 years old. It was the recipe of Aasta Kaasa Lotvedt, my grandmother, who came from Heddal, Telemark, Norway."

    ½ cup sugar
    ½ cup butter and lard, mixed
    1 egg, beaten
    1 cup molasses
    2½ cups sifted flour
    1½ tsp. soda
    1 tsp. cinnamon
    1 tsp. ginger
    ½ tsp. cloves
    ½ tsp. salt
    1 cup hot water

Cream sugar and shortening. Add beaten egg and molasses. Then add dry ingredients which have been sifted together. Add hot water last and beat until smooth. Bake in greased shallow pan at 350 degrees F. about 45-50 minutes. Makes 15 portions.

Babe Didriksen Zaharias

Babe Didriksen Zaharias, whose father Ole Didriksen was an immigrant from Norway, was honored as Woman Athlete of the First Half of the Twentieth Century. Born in 1912 in Port Arthur, Texas, she dominated women's events at the 1932 Olympics in Los Angeles. Although she excelled in many sports, basketball and golf were her specialties. She died of cancer in 1956.

Norwegian immigrants brought these 18th century silver fish servers, sugar spoons and ale tankard. Vesterheim collection.

Prince's Cake
Fyrstekake

Sigurd Daasvand of Brooklyn, N.Y., is former editor-in-chief of the Norwegian language newspaper Nordisk Tidende, *published every Thursday in Brooklyn. He was decorated by King Olav V of Norway with the St. Olav's Medal and by Nordmann-Forbundet (Norseman Federation) in Olso, Norway. He is a board member of the Norwegian-American Museum in Decorah, Iowa, and the Norwegian-American Historical Association in Northfield, Minn.*

1½ cups flour
1 tsp. baking powder
½ cup sugar
½ cup plus 1 Tbsp. butter
1 egg or 2 egg yolks
Almond filling:
   1 cup ground almonds
   1 cup powdered sugar
   2 egg whites, slightly beaten

Mix dry ingredients into mixing bowl. Blend in butter with pastry blender or with your fingertips until mixture resembles coarse flour. Thoroughly beat in egg or egg yolks. Chill well. If you wish blanched almonds, scald them. Unblanched give a better flavor. Grind almonds once, then grind a second time with powdered sugar. Blend thoroughly with beaten egg whites until mixture is firm and smooth. Chill.

Press 2/3 of the chilled dough into 8-inch round ungreased cake pan, covering bottom and sides. Spread almond mixture evenly over dough. Roll remainder of dough out to ⅛-inch thickness and cut into 8 strips ½ inch in width. Lay four of the strips parallel to each other across top of filling. Arrange remaining 4 strips at right angles, weaving to form a lattice pattern. Cut out another ½-inch wide strip and press around edge of cake. Brush with slightly beaten egg. Bake at 375 degrees F. for 25 to 30 minutes, or until golden brown and thoroughly baked. Leave cake on rack a few minutes before carefully loosening sides and removing from pan. Cut in wedges.

"This is good to serve for family and friends Saturday night or Sunday afternoon together with a nice cup of coffee and also at birthday parties. Our family is very fond of this cake. In fact, we grew up with it back home in Norway, where our mother used to bake it."

Else's Whipped Cream Layer Cake
Else's Bløtkake

Else Sevig, Minneapolis, and her husband Mike are Norwegian folksingers who have recorded several albums.

6 large eggs
¾ cup sugar
1 cup flour
Filling:
6 to 9 Tbsp. milk or half-and-half
4 cups whipping cream
1 Tbsp. powdered sugar
½ tsp. vanilla
1 to 2 cups berries or fruit (strawberries, pineapple, peaches or apricots) fresh or frozen, or 1 cup finely chopped walnuts

Beat eggs and sugar until stiff, about 10 minutes at high speed with electric mixer. Gently fold in sifted flour. Pour into 10-to-12-inch springform pan, the bottom greased and floured. If you use another type of pan, line bottom with wax paper. Bake in center of oven at 325 degrees F. about 30 minutes or until a toothpick inserted in center comes out clean. Leave oven door open two minutes before taking cake out of oven. When completely cool, remove cake from pan.

Cut cake in two or three layers, using a long, thin knife. Rotate the cake as you cut. Sprinkle three tablespoons milk or half-and-half over each layer. Whip the cream with powdered sugar and vanilla. Mix fruit, berries or nuts with two-thirds of the whipped cream mixture and spread between layers. Put remaining whipped cream on top and sides and use for decorating. Extra berries and fruit can also be added for decoration.

Cake can be filled the day before serving, in which case use less milk or half-and-half on each layer. Cover and store in cool place. This cake is used for Norwegian birthday parties, weddings or any festive occasion.

Whipped Cream Layer Cake
Norwegian Bløtkake

Lottie Huse Brown sends this recipe from Clifton, Texas, where there is a large Norwegian-American population. "When we visited Norway, this cake was served in practically every home. It is full of calories and very delicious."

4 cups flour
1 cup butter
2 tsp. baking powder
3 eggs
1 cup sugar
vanilla pudding
prepared whipped topping
jam, strawberries, sliced peaches, banana or pineapple chunks

Mix flour, butter and baking powder. In another bowl beat eggs; add sugar. Combine two mixtures and mix well. Knead. Divide into 9 sections and roll each to plate size. Bake on greased cookie sheet at 350 degrees F. 10-15 minutes, or until lightly browned. Use three layers for each cake. Put pudding and fruit between layers and cover with whipped topping. Decorate with fruit, nuts, coconut, etc.

Le Ann Wangsness-Bahr of Maple Grove, Minn., said after a trip abroad, "In Norway, Bløtkake is served at the table, where each piece is cut and placed on the plate. If the cake remains standing and you are single, you are soon to be married. A 10-year-old friend always tipped her piece over with her fork."

Knute Rockne

Knute Rockne, famed Notre Dame football coach, was born in Voss, Norway, in 1888, and lived in the United States from the age of 5. He played end for Notre Dame and coached from 1918 until his death in a plane crash in 1931. His teams won 105 games, lost 12 and tied 5. They were undefeated and untied national champions in 1919, 1920, 1924, 1929 and 1930.

Raspberry Cake
Bringebærkake

Marilyn Wang Engwall, Rochester, Minn. Her husband, Clarence W. Engwall, is a board member of Vesterheim. She says, "My Norsk grandmother came from Innset, Østerdal, and my Norsk grandfather from Os, Østerdal. I have visited both family farms, still owned by our relatives. Both farm homes still contain all the antique furniture and artifacts. Each family farm also has a sæter (mountain farm). My husband and I have been to Norway six times. This cake is typical of what is served there."

   1½ **cups flour**
   ½ **cup sugar**
   1 **tsp. baking powder**
   ½ **cup butter**
   1 **egg**
   ½ **cup raspberry jam, divided**
Filling:
   ½ **cup butter**
   2/3 **cup sugar**
   ½ **tsp. almond extract**
   2 **eggs**
   1 **cup finely ground blanched almonds (like coarse corn meal)**
Frosting:
   ½ **cup powdered sugar**
   2 **tsp. lemon juice**

Grease a 9"x1½" springform pan. Blend flour, sugar and baking powder. Add butter and mix as for pie crust. Add egg and blend with a fork until flour is moistened. Press dough evenly on bottom of pan. Spread ¼ cup raspberry jam over dough. Cover and chill while making filling.

For filling: Cream butter and sugar. Add extract. Add eggs one at a time, beating well. Mix in ground almonds. Spoon filling on top of jam. Bake at 350 degrees for 50 minutes. Cool in pan and remove cake carefully. Spread remaining ¼ cup jam over top. Mix powdered sugar and lemon juice together and drizzle on top of jam.

Can be made ahead of time and frozen.

Apple Cake
Eplekake

Mrs. Lawrence O. Hauge of Edina, Minn., writes: "My mother and father, both Norwegian immigrants, met in Minneapolis. Our home life was very Norwegian oriented for which I have been thankful."

   2 **eggs, well beaten**
   1½ **cups sugar, half brown and half white**
   2 **tsp. vanilla**
   1½ **cups flour**
   2 **tsp. baking powder**
   ¼ **tsp. salt**
   2½ **cups diced apples**
   ½ **cup coarsely broken nutmeats**

Beat eggs, sugar and vanilla together. Sift dry ingredients together and add to other mixture. Add apples and nuts. Bake in a 13x9-inch pan at 375 degrees F. for 30 to 35 minutes. Serve cold with whipped cream.

Mother's Sour Cream Frosting
Mors rømmekrem

Ruth Wickney of Northwood, N.D., writes: "This frosting on white or Lady Baltimore cake was made every other Saturday throughout my growing-up years. It was special and is remembered with nostalgia. (Alternate Saturdays it was chocolate cake!")

   4 **eggs or 5 yolks and 1 egg**
   1 **cup sugar**
   1 **cup sour cream**
   1 **tsp. almond extract**
   chopped nuts

Put eggs or yolks and one whole egg, sugar and sour cream in double boiler. Stir and cook until thick. Remove from burner and add almond extract. Frost cooled cake. Sprinkle with chopped nuts.

Norwegian Wedding Cake
Kransekake

Kransekake, or ring (tree) cake, is a festival tradition in Norway. It is served at Christmas because of its tree shape, at weddings because of its impressive height and for anniversaries and birthdays because of its many layers. It can be made in as many rings as there are years to observe.

It can be served as a bridegroom's cake at wedding receptions, where each guest is given a small piece in addition to the regular cake.

The cake is so decorative that some people use it as a centerpiece and bake extra rings for serving. The cake tower is hollow, so a bottle of wine can be hidden inside as an extra treat after the cake is eaten.

Although the recipe for *kransekake* is simple, you may want to bake a few practice rings before you attempt the "real thing." Try half a recipe to learn the cutting and baking techniques.

Here are two versions of *kransekake* from Decorah, Iowa, cooks. The first has a light delicate flavor and a chewy, cookie-like texture. It is baked in 18 concentric ring mold pans. These pans are available at Scandinavian specialty shops. Local bakeries can usually provide the almond paste.

The second recipe is made of a rich cookie dough with the taste of a butter or *spritz* cookie. It is baked on 26 squares of aluminum-wrapped cardboard. This is the answer for those who do not want to invest in the ring mold pans.

Both recipes produce baked rings that are stacked to make this conical cake with a hollow center. To serve, simply lift off each layer and break into serving-size pieces.

Arla Erickson Lyon's Recipe

- 1 lb. almond paste
- 1 lb. powdered sugar, sifted
- 2 egg whites, unbeaten
- ¼ cup powdered sugar for kneading

Mix almond paste and powdered sugar. Add egg whites. Mix well. Place bowl in hot water and knead dough until it is lukewarm. Turn out on board sprinkled with ¼ cup powdered sugar. Let rest 10 minutes.

Knead 2 to 3 minutes. Press dough through cookie press into greased ring forms. Bake at 300 degrees F. for 20 minutes. Do not remove rings from forms until cold. Place rings on top of one another, icing each one with frosting as you stack them.

Frosting:
- 1½ cups powdered sugar, sifted
- 1 egg white, unbeaten
- 1 tsp. vinegar

Mix well and drizzle over cake rings. Arla sometime stacks five or six rings and freezes them. Later she stacks the rest of them to complete the cake. The rings freeze well.

She says, "My husband used an electric drill to remove the points of the star on my cookie press so this enables me to press dough out faster. Or, you can roll out by hand and lay in the pans. But if you are making seven pounds at a time, you try to find the easiest way."

If you do not wish to make the recipe into rings, you can cut into rectangles for cookies and frost them.

Norma Wangsness's Kransekake

- 2 cups soft butter
- 1 cup almond paste
- 2 cups sifted powdered sugar
- 2 tsp. almond extract
- 4 egg yolks
- 5 cups sifted flour

It will take 1½ recipes to make the total 26-ring cake.

Cream together until smooth the butter, almond paste, powdered sugar and almond extract. Beat egg yolks in well. Measure flour after it has been sifted and add gradually, mixing until very smooth.

Place paper patterns on lightly greased cookie sheets. Put dough into cookie press or pastry bag. Press out to shape

Olsen's Bakery, 5722 8th Avenue, Brooklyn, N.Y., is famous for its kransekake. The bakery is owned and operated by Thoralf Olsen. Three Olsen sons work with him. Pictured are, left to right, Roy, Brian and Thoralf Olsen, John Nilsen and Kenneth Olsen.

Their recipe calls for almond paste, rye flour, sugar and egg whites. A tip from the baker: "After fitting dough in rings, cut ends with knife and butt edges to form a perfect circle. This will assure a balanced finished product."
Darrell Henning photograph.

rings around *inside* edges of paper patterns. Chill 15 minutes if desired.

Bake in oven at 350 degrees F. 15 minutes or until very lightly browned. Cool on paper pattern.

To assemble cake, drizzle some frosting on platter. This will anchor cake. Place largest ring on frosting. Apply frosting in scallops on first ring. Place next largest ring on top and decorate and stack in order until you have used all 26 layers. The scalloped frosting will hold each ring in place.

Frosting:
1½ cups sifted powdered sugar
1 egg white
1 tsp. vinegar

Stir together. If not stiff enough, add more powdered sugar. Put in pastry tube with small round tip.

To decorate, use small Norwegian flags on stick pins and insert in cake. Or buy marzipan fruits and stick on toothpicks. Slide toothpicks between layers to hold in place. Or wrap tiny presents or notes and decorate for a birthday party.

To serve, break into 2½-inch pieces. Makes about 60-75 broken pieces. "For each of my daughters' weddings, I made five of these. Two of the five were used as centerpieces with one behind to use for the actual serving. We used Norwegian flags to decorate and placed the cakes on Norwegian blue plates with fresh ivy and baby's breath around the base."

Evonne Anderson of Moorhead, Minn., says, "In Norway this is also used for confirmations and graduations."

Cardboard Paper Patterns

You will need to cut 26 squares of cardboard. The first will be a 2-inch square, the second a 2¼-inch square, etc., each one ¼ inch larger than the one before. The 26th layer square will be 8¼ inches square. Cover each square with heavy duty aluminum wrap, covering completely to prevent scorching.

Using a compass, make a circle one inch in diameter on the #1 square, on #2 a 1¼-inch circle, etc., until #26 which will be 7¼ inches in diameter. Number each pattern to keep them in order.

Source: Kransekake ring pans and almond paste may be purchased at Maid of Scandinavia, 14150 Nicolet Ave. S., Minneapolis, Mn. 55403.

Cookies

Drop Cookies
Gudbrandsdalkaker

Rolf H. Erickson of Evanston, Ill., is on the board of directors of the Norwegian-American Museum and the Norwegian-American Historical Association.

He writes: "My mother's Aunt Berit Ramseth Jacobson introduced me to the Gudbrandsdal cookie 33 years ago. As a child of eight, I stuffed myself with them on a Christmas visit to her home in Milwaukee, Wis.

"Highly pleased that I liked her baking, she filled my pockets for the trip home, admonishing me to remember that the Gudbrandsdal cookie was her mother's recipe and had been made and served at their home in Tynset, Østerdal.

"As an adult I learned that Great-grandmother Barbro, unable to afford almonds after her arrival in Wisconsin in 1888, substituted hickory nuts—free for the gathering from farm woodlots.

"In 1970, Borghild Ramseth Nissen found in an old family cookbook that almonds were the original ingredient. So the genuine Gudbrandsdal again appears on Ramseth Christmas tables."

- 1 cup sugar
- 1 cup vegetable shortening, butter or margarine
- 1 cup cornstarch
- 2 cups flour
- 1 cup whipping cream
  few drops almond flavoring
- 1 cup sliced almonds

Blend sugar and shortening. Add rest of ingredients in order, blending after each addition. This is a drop cookie and should not be larger than a half-dollar.

Bake in slow oven at 250 degrees F. until cookie is light golden brown around edges and white in center.

Butter Rings
Berlinerkranser

Eleanor Anundsen of Decorah sent this recipe, which was handed down from her husband's grandmother, Helma Anundsen. Helma's husband, B. Anundsen, was founder (1874) and publisher of the Norwegian newspaper Decorah-Posten. *In the 1920s, the* Decorah-Posten *had a circulation of 45,000. It was consolidated in 1972 with* Western Viking *of Seattle, Wash.*

- 3 hard-boiled egg yolks
- 4 raw egg yolks
- 1 cup plus 2 Tbsp. sugar
- 5 to 5½ cups flour
- 1 pound butter
- 1 egg white

Mash yolks of hard-boiled eggs. Add yolks of raw eggs, blending into a smooth paste. Add sugar, beating well. Add flour and butter alternately, using your hands. Roll pieces of dough to the thickness of a pencil, about three inches long. Shape each like a bow. Whip egg white and brush on top of each cookie. Bake at 350 degrees F. until light golden brown. Makes about seven dozen cookies. "We still use this recipe at Christmas time. They should be stored in a cool place. They also freeze well."

Sonja Henie

Norwegian-born Sonja Henie (1912-69) won the Olympic Games figure-skating championship in 1928, 1932 and 1936. She won ten world championships from 1927 through 1936, was the star of the Hollywood Ice Review for 18 years, and had a leading role in several motion pictures. She became an American citizen in 1941. With her husband, she left the people of Norway a major museum of modern art in suburban Oslo.

Poor Man's Cakes
Fattigmann

Helen M. Haatvedt of Decorah says: "My grandmother and my mother, both of whom were experts at making this cookie, insisted that it be handled very carefully and not allowed to be fried too dark or not browned enough. The cookies had to be uniform in size and thickness and could not be tough from too much stirring. This recipe goes back to 1882."

```
1 whole egg
3 egg yolks
4 Tbsp. cream
4 tsp. sugar
1 Tbsp. melted butter
¼ tsp. ground cardamom
1½ cups flour, approximately
```

Beat egg and egg yolks slightly. Add other ingredients. Use enough flour to make a soft dough. Mix, handling as little and as lightly as possible. Roll out on floured cloth and cut in 2" X 2" diamond shapes. Fry in hot lard until very lightly browned. Drain on brown paper and dust with powdered sugar when cool.

Kringle

Marilyn Haugen Istad of Decorah, Iowa, says: "This is the recipe used by my daughter Jan and her teenage friends about 13 years ago to make kringle. As a demonstration in a store window for the Nordic Fest, they rolled and baked these tasty goodies and sold them to the visitors."

```
5¼ cups flour
 2 tsp. baking powder
   pinch salt
2/3 cup margarine
 2 cups sugar
 1 tsp. vanilla
 2 egg yolks, unbeaten
 2 cups buttermilk
 2 tsp. soda
```

Mix flour, baking powder and salt and set aside. Cream margarine, sugar and vanilla. Add egg yolks. Add soda to buttermilk and add to creamed mixture before foaming stops. Add dry ingredients Chill at least 3 hours.

Place a clean dish towel on flat surface. Flour well. Drop a teaspoonful of dough onto floured towel. Roll into a long rope, about 6 inches long and ⅜ inch in diameter. Place on greased cookie sheets, making figure 8s or pretzel design with the dough rope.

Bake 4 minutes on bottom shelf of oven, move to top shelf and bake 2 minutes longer until lightly browned on bottom.

Anise Kringle

Dagney Johansen gave this traditional Norwegian cookie recipe to the Nordic Heritage Museum of Seattle, whose director is Marianne Forssblad. The Museum, small and growing, represents all Scandinavian heritage. Honorary trustees include the consuls of Norway, Sweden, Finland, Iceland and Denmark.

```
1½ cups granulated sugar
 1 cup butter or shortening
 1 whole egg
 4 egg yolks
 ½ tsp. baking powder
 2 heaping tsp. anise seed
 3 cups white flour
```

Mix all ingredients, in order given, in one bowl. Roll small amounts of dough to pencil thickness. Cut into 8- or 9-inch lengths. Form into pretzel shapes. Arrange on a greased cookie sheet and bake at 350 degrees F. until light brown. Makes about four dozen.

Performers

Well-known actresses and actors of Norwegian descent include Celeste Holm, Arlene Dahl, Liv Ullman, Peggy Lee (born Norma Delores Egstrom), Peter Graves and James Arness.

Rosettes

Lloyd George Melgard of Warren, Minn., describes himself as a retired farmer, world traveler, correspondent, happy bachelor and a collector of cookbooks, interested in fine antiques and porcelains. He has published a history of his community. "My father's three uncles and an aunt came to Black River Falls, Wis., from the Melgard Farm in Sør Fron above Hundorp in Gudbrandsdal around the time of the Civil War."

- 2 eggs
- 1 tsp. sugar
- ¼ tsp. salt
- 1 cup milk
- 1 cup flour

Beat eggs slightly with sugar and salt. Add milk and flour and beat until smooth. Heat rosette iron in hot lard or vegetable shortening to 370 degrees F. For the first rosette, wipe excess fat from iron with paper towels and dip into batter, but do not allow to come over top of iron. Return iron to hot fat and immerse. Fry for about 20 seconds or until color desired.

In removing iron from fat, turn it over to drain. Jolt rosette off iron and repeat. If rosette falls off iron in hot fat, you do not have enough flour in batter. If rosette is thick, you have too much flour and need to thin a bit with milk.

This recipe makes 40 rosettes. When you are finished cooking rosettes, place them on paper towels on a cookie sheet with towels between each layer. Put in oven at 300 degrees F. Turn off heat. Allow to cool. This will remove excess fat from rosettes and improve them. They may be dusted with powdered sugar before serving. In Norway they are sometimes stacked three high with whipped cream between them and then topped with fruit.

"I have used this recipe for years with good results. I make it for giving to many families at Christmas time. My home reeks of Crisco after completing that project, and my feet hurt from standing and frying the rosettes one at a time."

Ethelyn Thompson of Hollandale, Wis.; Hazel Hove Hendrickson of Ossian, Iowa; and Bernice Oellien of Madison, Minn.; also sent in recipes for rosettes. Ethelyn Thompson wrote: "During my years of guiding at Little Norway, I developed an interest in Norwegian stave churches. It took me three trips to Norway to see all 31 of them."

Frycakes
American "Smultringer"

This recipe was sent in by Barbara Hanson Bulman, Forest City, Ia. for her 96-year-old mother, Gina J. Hanson Hanson, Forest City, Iowa. Her son, John K. Hanson, is chairman of the board and chief executive officer of Winnebago Industries, Inc., of Forest City.

- 1/3 cup shortening
- 1 cup sugar
- 2 eggs
- 1 cup milk
- 4 cups flour
- 4 tsp. baking powder
- ¼ tsp. nutmeg
  pinch salt
- ½ tsp. lemon extract
  oil for frying

Cream shortening and sugar; add eggs. Sift together dry ingredients and add alternately with milk to first mixture. Add flavoring. Mix well, but be careful not to overmix or to use too much flour. Chill dough for ease in rolling. Divide dough into two portions for rolling. Work on board with just enough flour to roll fairly thick. Cut with doughnut cutter and fry in hot oil at 370 degrees F. Turn cakes only once, when top shows cracks. Drain on paper towels.

Pretzel

In Norway, the baker's sign is a large pretzel.

The Princess

Princess Sonja of Norway was a special guest at a Vesterheim celebration at the Minneapolis Institute of Art Nov. 4, 1979. Women of the Norman Lodge #41, Madison, Minn., baked the cookies that were served.

When Norwegian cooks serve coffee after dinner, seven is considered the magic number for the variety of cookies to accompany it. The seven selected by the Madison women were *fattigmann, krumkaker, rosettes, Berlinerkranser, sandbakkels, spritz* and *goro*.　　Rude photo

Wafer Cones or Crumb Cake
Krumkake

Le Ann Wangsness-Bahr of Maple Grove, Minn. "The trick to eating krumkake *is to insert the tip of your tongue in open center to bite off a piece. Otherwise, crumb cake!"*

- **3 eggs, well beaten**
- **½ cup sugar**
- **½ cup melted butter**
- **¼ tsp. salt**
- **½ cup flour**
- **1 tsp. flavoring (almond and lemon extract)**

Beat eggs well. Add sugar, melted butter, salt and flavoring. Beat well. Stir in flour.

Heat *krumkake* iron on medium heat. Put a teaspoonful of batter on iron. Bake one minute or less, turn iron over and bake until very lightly browned. Remove from iron and quickly roll on cone-shape form. Store in tight container.

Immigration

In proportion to its population, Norway has sent more of its people to live in America than any other country except Ireland.

Stryl
A *type of* krumkake

Ann Urness Gesme and her husband, Dean, of Cedar Rapids, Iowa, are "Norwegian all the way." All 8 of her great-grandparents came from Norway, Sogning on her father's side and Valdres on her mother's. Dean is secretary of Bygdelagenes Fellesraad, National Council of Bygdelags. In early 20th century America, Norwegian immigrants whose roots were in the same district in Norway organized into bygdelags. Dean is president of Vestlandslaget, a national organization of four different bygdelags.

- **¾ cup sugar**
- **1½ cups flour**
- **½ tsp. ground cardamom**
- **1 cup whipping cream**
- **½ cup half-and-half**
- **½ cup milk**

Mix sugar, flour and cardamom. Add whipping cream and stir in. Stir in half-and-half and then the milk. Bake on *krumkake* iron.

Increase the amount of half-and-half and decrease the amount of milk if a richer krumkake is desired. A bit of melted butter added will do the same thing. "The absence of butter and eggs makes this recipe unique. It's my favorite *krumkake* recipe."

Goro

Lillian Pederson of Marietta, Minn., sent this recipe for one variety of cookie served to Princess Sonja of Norway.

- 3 eggs
- 1 cup sugar
- 1 cup sweet cream
- 1 cup melted butter
- 2½ cups flour
- 1 tsp. cinnamon or ¼ tsp. ground cardamom

Beat eggs well, add sugar and blend thoroughly. Add cream, melted butter, then sifted dry ingredients and mix. Roll out thin and cut out, using paper pattern to fit a goro iron. Place on heated iron; turn to bake other side. After removing goro, cut in thirds while still warm. Store in air-tight container or a dry area.

Olive Nordby of Madison, Wis., uses cardamom in her goro cookies. She says: "The best cardamom comes in seed form, sold in bulk at herb or health food stores. Remove seed from pods and crush with mortar and pestle. Since it is important to have the dough cold, it helps to have two people working, one taking sections from refrigerator and baking and the other cutting apart and stacking them."

Spiced Hermits

Marilyn Skaugstad of Iowa City, Iowa

- 1 cup shortening
- 2 cups sugar
- 3 eggs
- 1 tsp. cinnamon
- 1 tsp. nutmeg
- ½ tsp. cloves
- 2 tsp. lemon extract
- 1 tsp. soda dissolved in 1 Tbsp. hot water
- 2 cups raisins, rinsed and ground
- 3½ cups all-purpose flour

Combine ingredients in order given and chill dough. Roll out thinly and cut with large round cookie cutter. Sprinkle with sugar and bake at 350 degrees F. for 10 to 12 minutes. Makes a large batch.

Grandma Rosdail's Cookies
Oldemors kaker

This recipe comes from Rachel O. Southcombe of Newark, Ill., whose great-grandfather was Daniel Stenson Rosdail. He was one-sixth owner of the Restauration and had the largest family on board, seven including the parents. "The woman the cookies are named after was the widow of John Rosdail, who came to America in 1825 on board the sloop Restauration."

- 1½ cups raisins, boiled
- 1 cup butter, or other shortening
- 2 cups sugar
- 2 eggs, beaten
- 1 cup, minus 2 Tbsp., sour milk
- 1 tsp. soda
- 1 tsp. vanilla
- 2½ to 3 cups flour
- 1 tsp. baking powder

Boil raisins in just enough water to cover. Sweeten and cool. Drain.

Cream butter and sugar. Add beaten eggs. Add soda to sour milk and stir. Add sour milk and soda to first mixture. Add cooled raisins and vanilla. Add baking powder and enough flour to handle when rolling out.

Roll out on floured board and cut with cookie cutter. Place on greased cookie sheets. Bake at 350 to 375 degrees F. until light brown.

Early Gods

The chief gods of Norwegian antiquity were Odin, god of war and wisdom; Thor, the god of good crops, and an ardent slayer of trolls and giants; and Frey, associated with fertility. Later, there were Balder, the bright and good god, and Loke, the bad half-god. These gods played an important part in Norwegian mythology that has been handed down from pre-Christian times.

This miniature Viking ship of enamel in a filigree frame represents a technique known as *plique-á-jour* for which Norway was famous at the turn of the century. The ship was contributed to the Vesterheim collection by Estelle Knudsen of Eden Prairie, Minn., and her sister Margaret Smaby of Minneapolis, Minn., in memory of their mother, Amelia Holm-Hagen. The ship was exhibited in three American cities in a show, "The Art of Norway."

Sandbakkels

Lois Wold Christenson of Decorah, Iowa, a third generation Norwegian, whose family sings as the "Christenson Family Singers," sends this recipe. She and her husband Paul, who is pastor of First Lutheran Church, have six children. They have performed on three Scandinavian and European tours, and at the annual Nordic Fest.

> **2 cups shortening (1 cup butter and 1 cup margarine)**
> **1 cup sugar**
> **6 Tbsp. whipping cream**
> **1 Tbsp. brandy (or brandy flavoring)**
> **1 egg**
> **6 cups flour**

Cream shortening and sugar. Add cream, brandy and egg. Slowly add flour until all is well mixed. Chill slightly before pressing in tins.

Roll into small balls. Press into sandbakkel tins and keep pressing until thin layer covers bottom and sides. Trim off excess from edges.

Bake at 350 degrees F. until light golden in color.

"You can purchase sandbakkel tins at Scandinavian shops. This recipe freezes well. It's delicious when filled with fruit, pie filling, etc., and topped with whipped cream, but also great plain."

Sandbakkels

Gyda Paulson-Thoen Mahlum of Beloit, Wis., won a gold medal in rosemaling in 1972 and has studied with teachers from Norway. Three examples of her rosemaling were in the traveling exhibit in Norway in 1975. Several pieces of her work have been purchased by the Norwegian-American Museum in Decorah, Iowa. She is a member of the Valdres Samband and Hadeland Lag.

> **½ cup butter**
> **½ cup vegetable shortening**
> **¾ cup sugar**
> **1 egg**
> **1 tsp. vanilla**
> **¼ tsp. almond extract**
> **2¼ cups flour**

Cream shortenings and sugar; add egg and flavorings and beat well. Sift flour and gradually add to creamed mixture. Mix well. Turn dough onto waxed paper and wrap. Chill in refrigerator for about 45 minutes. Preheat oven to 350 degrees F. Cut thin slices of dough and press into sandbakkel tins, beginning at the bottom and working upward to the top edge of the tin so it will not be too thick at the bottom. If dough becomes a little sticky, flour your fingers lightly.

Place on cookie sheet and bake for 15 minutes or until golden brown. Baking time may vary with the size of the tin. Cool in tins. When cool turn to release the sandbakkels. If necessary, tap the tin very gently. Makes 5 dozen.

Christmas Tarts

Dorothy Erickson Norby of Mabel, Minn., writes: "These cookies have always been served in my home starting with Thanksgiving and continuing through the Christmas season. My Norwegian grandmother started the custom. They are quite a lot of work, but well worth it."

1 cup whipping cream
3 cups flour, approximately
1 cup *unsalted* butter
   red-colored sugar for sprinkling

Pour cream into a small mixing bowl. Add 1 cup flour or a little more. Mix and turn out on a floured pastry canvas. Dough will be soft and sticky. Roll out, adding more flour as necessary, and add little chunks of butter. Double over, roll, add more butter, double over, roll, etc., until all the butter has been used.

"Pick up the dough and throw it on your counter a few times. This sounds silly, but I don't dare *not* do it!"

Chill the dough.

Using a small amount of dough at a time, roll out quite thin using as little flour as possible. Cut into diamond shapes about 2" x 3". Sprinkle heavily with red sugar. Bake at 400 degrees F. 7 to 8 minutes, chilling cookie sheet between each baking. Do not overbake, as the tops must not be brown.

Makes about 5 dozen. Store in a large flat box. Do not freeze. Keep in a dry, cool place.

Polar Explorer

Roald Amundsen (1872-1928) devoted his life to polar exploration. On December 14, 1911, he discovered the South Pole and planted the Norwegian flag there. In 1903-1906, he sailed the sloop *Gjoa* from the Atlantic to the Pacific via the Northwest Passage. In 1926 he flew over the North Pole in the dirigible *Norge*. His autobiography was titled *My Life as an Explorer*. Amundsen and five others died on an air rescue mission into the Arctic in 1928.

Spritz

Irene O. Engebretson of Decorah, Iowa.

1 cup butter or margarine
2/3 cup sugar
3 egg yolks
1 tsp. almond extract
½ tsp. vanilla
2½ cups flour

Cream shortening and sugar. Add egg yolks and extracts. Mix well. Add flour and mix well. Press dough onto cookie sheets through spritz cookie tube into different designs. Bake in oven at 350 degrees F. until light golden brown.

Almond Candy
Marsipan

Sigurd Daasvand of Oslo, Norway.

1 lb. sweet almonds, scalded
¼ lb. bitter almonds
1 lb. powdered sugar
1 Tbsp. egg white
   food coloring

Grind almonds and bitter almonds finely, three or four times. Gradually work into the mixture the powdered sugar and egg white, as necessary.

When dough is smooth and workable, form into tiny loaves of bread, potatoes, fruits, vegetables or flowers, and color with food coloring. Use cocoa to color potatoes, and prick with toothpick. Strawberries look pretty with artificial leaves added.

Or color several lumps of the dough in different colors, roll them out with rolling pin, brush lightly with egg white and place one on top of the other. Then cut in small squares or diamonds, and each piece will contain several beautiful colored layers. Candy may also be coated with chocolate.

Desserts

Fruit Soup or Sweet Soup
Søtsuppe

Gretchen Hansen Quie of St. Paul, Minn., the First Lady of Minnesota, and her husband, Albert, governor of Minnesota, both have Norwegian backgrounds. The governor's family comes from Hallingdal and Mrs. Quie's family from the Stavanger fjord area. Mrs. Quie writes: "Al's Norwegian mother introduced me to søtsuppe or sweet soup and this is my approximation of her recipe. She always had raspberries in her garden and their addition makes it truly "Nettie's delight."

1 cup pitted prunes
1 cup raisins
1 cup chopped peeled apple
1 Tbsp. finely chopped orange peel
1 orange, peeled and cut up
4 cups water
1 Tbsp. lemon juice
¼ cup sugar (or more)
1 stick cinnamon
¼ tsp. salt
2 Tbsp. quick-cooking tapioca
1 10-oz. pkg. frozen raspberries

Combine all ingredients except tapioca and raspberries in large saucepan. Simmer for 1 hour. Sprinkle tapioca over soup and stir to avoid lumping. Cook 15 minutes more. Cool a few minutes. Add frozen raspberries and stir occasionally until they are thawed. Serve hot, or chill and serve with whipped cream. Makes 8 to 10 servings.

Names

Many Norwegian surnames are based on the name of the farm where the family lived, so there is a touch of the outdoors to many family names. For instance, *dal* means valley, *vik* is bay, *haug* is hill, *rud* clearing, *stad* place, *holm,* island, *vaag* inlet, and *berg* cliff.

Sweet Soup
Søtsuppe

Sonja Strom Scarseth of Aurora, Ill., writes: "My husband Bill and I think it's lucky that our families came from the same area in Norway. It saves so many arguments. We both like Berlinerkranser instead of kringle, we both pour melted butter on our lutefisk instead of cream sauce, we both use grape juice in our søtsuppe. Our only point of difference: I put sugar on my lefse, and he thinks that is perfectly horrible! 'You wouldn't put sugar on mashed potatoes, would you?' Well, you do have to have something to argue about."

4 cups cranberry-grape juice
1 lemon, thinly sliced
2/3 cup sugar, approximately
1 stick cinnamon, approximately 1½ inches long
1 cup raisins
¼ tsp. salt
2 Tbsp. quick-cooking tapioca

Combine all ingredients except tapioca in saucepan. Bring to a boil, then cover and simmer 15-20 minutes, or until lemon rind is tender and semi-transparent. Add tapioca and boil 2 to 3 minutes, or until tapioca is clear. Soup will still be runny when cool.

Leave the lemon in the soup; it is to be eaten, too. Serve in a sauce dish with Norwegian Christmas cookies. May be served warm, room temperature or chilled. Serves 8 to 10. Can be frozen 6-12 months. Thaw and reheat to recombine ingredients.

Vacation

In Norway July is vacation month. Most businesses close down for a three-week period.

Prune Soup
Suiskesuppe

Ruth Christoffer Carlsen of Iowa City writes: "My family's story begins in Laerdal, a fishing village at the end of the Sognefjord. My great-grandfather, Kris Kristofferson, did not return from the sea one night and a morning search found him dead in his boat. My great-grandmother, Brita, realized that her five little boys would have no future in Laerdal. What would she live on? So, selling everything possible to finance the trip, she came to Stoughton, Wis., in 1867 with Big Chris, Little Chris, Big Pete, Little Pete and Lickey.

"The spelling of the name was changed at Ellis Island to Christoffer. Only three of the boys survived: Big Chris, my grandfather; Little Chris and Lickey.

"Grandfather never forgot a young girl he had known in Laerdal and when he had saved enough money he went back to claim her as his bride and brought her back to Stoughton. Her name was Mari Forthün.

"This is one of her recipes which my mother always served on Good Friday. Though called a soup, it was used as a dessert in our home."

1 pound prunes
4 Tbsp. sago*
1 stick cinnamon
1 can pie cherries
1 tsp. lemon juice
  sugar

Soak prunes, then boil in water to cover until soft. Remove pits and return prunes to liquid. Add sago and cinnamon stick. Cook until thickened. Add cherries and lemon juice. Sweeten to taste. Serve in bowls with plain cream.

*Sago is a thickening agent used widely in Scandinavian countries. It must be soaked an hour, and then drained, before using. It is not readily available in U.S. supermarkets and tapioca may be substituted for it.

Fruit Soup
Søtsuppe

Evonne Anderson of Moorhead, Minn.

¼ cup sago, soaked in water a few hours
2 cups pitted dried prunes
1 cup dried apricots
1 cup raisins
1 cup dried apple slices
1 stick cinnamon
1 cup grape juice

Combine in a saucepan the sago (after it has been soaked) and its water, dried fruits, cinnamon and grape juice. Bring to boil, then lower heat and simmer gently until the dried fruits are tender but not falling apart, about 30 minutes. Cool.

If you want it sweeter than the natural sugar in the fruit, add sugar or honey to taste. Can be served warm or cold. Makes 12 servings.

Rhubarb Fruit Soup
Rabarbrasuppe

Barbara Hamre Berg of Decorah, Iowa, writes: "I found this recipe in a magazine many years ago. Fruit soups are very Scandinavian."

1 11-oz. can mandarin oranges, including syrup
½ cup sugar
3 cups rhubarb, preferably red, cut in ½-inch pieces

Drain oranges, reserving syrup. In a one-quart saucepan, combine reserved syrup, sugar and rhubarb. Bring to a boil, cover and cook over low heat until rhubarb is tender, but still retains its shape, about 5 minutes. Remove from heat, stir in mandarin oranges. Chill.

Spoon into sherbet dishes. Serve with whipped cream, if desired. Serves four.

"I prefer no cream. I make it one batch at a time. It freezes very well and we like it with ice crystals still in it."

Norwegian Fruit Soup
Søtsuppe

Marilyn Skaugstad of Iowa City.

- **1 cup pitted prunes**
- **1 cup white or dark seedless raisins or a mixture**
- **½ cup currants**
- **2 cups chopped rhubarb**
- **3 cups water**
- **1 cup sugar**
- **½ cup quick-cooking tapioca**
- **1 stick cinnamon**
- **¼ tsp. salt**
- **2 cups grape juice (or part grape wine)**
- **juice of 1 lemon**

Combine all ingredients except grape juice and lemon juice. Bring to a slow boil. Turn down heat, cover and simmer until tapioca is clear. Stir frequently to keep tapioca from sticking to bottom of pan. Add grape juice and lemon juice and again bring to a boil. Serve hot or cold.

"It can be served with milk or cream for breakfast. It makes 10 to 12 small servings."

Hagletta

Erma W. Fruland of Newark, Ill., is the great-great-granddaughter of Daniel Stenson Rosdail, who was part owner of the sloop Restauration *which brought the first Norwegian emigrants to this country in 1825.*

- **2 quarts milk**
- **5 eggs, beaten**
- **1 cup sugar**
- **salt**
- **4 cups buttermilk**

Bring milk to a slow boil. Mix well-beaten eggs, sugar, salt and buttermilk. Add all at once to boiling milk. Do not stir until mixture has formed curds on top. Break, then fold over gently with a large spatula. Let boil slowly for about 40 minutes. Chill. Serve when ice cold.

Barbara Hamre Berg of Decorah, Iowa, contributed her version of Hagletta and said: "It is traditionally served at the end of a meal, but I like a large bowl of it for breakfast! I believe it is a recipe from the coastal areas of Norway because it has no counterpart in the Valdres area of Norway from where my ancestors came."

Lemon Custard in Cups
Citron pudding i kopper

Linda Wangsness Triebes, Des Moines, Iowa, writes: "I am a full-blooded Norwegian, married to David Triebes, with a two-year-old son Erik. I stay home to care for my son and work on my art, Norwegian rosemaling, gnome art and children's art. Most of my activities center on my strong Norwegian background, from traveling to Norway to continuing to meet Norwegian friends to keeping my family's heritage alive.

"This recipe came from my grandmother, Christina Lotvedt Anderson of Decorah, Iowa, my hometown. She was a boarding house cook, school cook and restaurant owner, which gave her the reputation as the best cook around."

- **2 Tbsp. butter**
- **1 cup sugar**
- **3 eggs, separated**
- **4 Tbsp. flour**
- **¼ tsp. salt**
- **5 Tbsp. lemon juice**
- **rind of 1 lemon**
- **1½ cups milk**

Cream butter, sugar and egg yolks and beat thoroughly. Add flour, salt, lemon juice and rind. Add milk. Fold in stiffly beaten egg whites. Pour into greased custard cups. Set cups in pan of water, approximately ¼ to ½ inch deep and bake 45 minutes at 350 degrees F. When done, each cup will contain custard at the bottom and sponge cake on top. Makes 8 servings.

Country and City Rømmegrøt
Rømmegrøt

Hilda Nelson of Fergus Falls, Minn., mother of Marion Nelson, director of the Norwegian-American Museum in Decorah, Iowa, sent recipes for two versions of the popular dish, Rømmegrøt. Hilda spent her childhood in Norway. She says, "No measurements were used for the many kinds of grøt. True country rømmegrøt was made with very thick sour cream. City rømmegrøt was made like drawn butter gravy, except thicker. It was made from butter instead of cream. Modern Norwegian-Americans prefer sweet rather than sour cream."

Country Rømmegrøt
3 cups sour cream
2 cups flour
2¼ quarts boiling milk
1 tsp. salt

Boil cream ½ hour; sift in flour gradually, stirring constantly. As the butter comes out, take off with a spoon and add rest of flour. Thin with boiling milk. Boil, remove from heat and add salt.

City Rømmegrøt
1 quart milk, scalded
½ cup butter or margarine
1 cup flour
1 tsp. salt
5 Tbsp. sugar
cinnamon

Melt butter or margarine in a heavy pan. Add 1 cup flour slowly as when making cream sauce. Watch carefully so that it doesn't scorch. Add scalded milk a little at a time. Mix and beat until smooth and thick. Add salt and sugar. Mix and pour into serving dish. Sprinkle sugar and cinnamon on top. Serve with melted butter on the side.

Evonne Anderson of Moorhead, Minn., wrote: "The pioneers used this as a main dish; today's Norwegians have a small dish for dessert. It can be made with milk if you don't want it so rich. My husband's grandfather homesteaded in western North Dakota, and he said they even made it with water when they didn't have milk. (That doesn't sound very good!)"

Cream Pudding
Fløtegrøt

Thora Leonard of Story City, Iowa, whose parents were born in Norway, says: "I grew up in an American home with beautiful Norwegian accents, as well as truly loyal American ideals!

"This pudding was called senje mat in the Norwegian community in which I lived as a child. It was customary for ladies to prepare this delicacy to take to a new mother in the neighborhood. Mothers then were confined to bed for longer periods of time after a baby was born, and babies were born at home. So, women were frequently seen carrying a bowl of senje mat (bed food) into a friend's house."

4 cups sweet cream
1 cup flour
2 cups warm milk
½ tsp. salt
sugar, cinnamon, raisins as topping

Bring cream to a boil. Let boil for 10 minutes. Simmer slowly while sifting flour into cream. Stir constantly until smooth and thick. When butterfat appears, remove it and save to use as a topping. Add warm milk, stirring to prevent scorching. Keep beating until mixture appears smooth and velvety. Add salt and continue stirring for about a minute.

"Pour into your prettiest china bowl and serve hot, topped with the butterfat which you dipped from the pudding as it was boiling. Add sugar, cinnamon and/or raisins, making a delicious and attractive topping for this special Norwegian dessert. It makes about six generous servings."

Old-Fashioned Custard Pudding with Oranges
Gammeldags krempudding med appelsiner

John K. Hanson, founder of Winnebago Industries, Inc., in Forest City, Iowa.

4 cups milk
3 eggs, lightly beaten
2 Tbsp. cornstarch
¾ cup sugar
1 tsp. vanilla
2 to 3 oranges, peeled and diced

Scald milk in top of double boiler. In mixing bowl, beat eggs. In small bowl, mix cornstarch and sugar. Add to beaten eggs. Pour scalded milk over eggs, cornstarch and sugar, stirring constantly. Return to top of double boiler and cook until custard adheres to spoon and is smooth.

Add vanilla. Put orange pieces in large serving bowl. Pour pudding over, mix gently and allow to cool.

"This is a delicious and nourishing family favorite. Mom served it family style in the traditional Bavarian china bowl with fruit painted on the base (one of her wedding presents) as a noon-time dessert."

Government Service

Two Minnesotans of Norwegian descent have served in recent years as vice-president of the United States. Hubert Horatio Humphrey (1911-1978) was elected in 1964 when Lyndon Johnson was elected president. Walter F. Mondale served from 1977 to 1981 when Jimmy Carter was president.

Two U.S. government officials of Norwegian extraction were Earl Warren, Chief Justice of the Supreme Court, and Karl Rølvaag, son of author Ole Rølvaag and former governor of Minnesota, who served as ambassador to Iceland under President Lyndon Johnson.

Rice Pudding
Risengrynsgrøt

Inez G. Schaefer of Rochester, Minn., is a member of the board of directors of the Norwegian-American Museum.

1 cup water
½ cup long-grained rice
½ tsp. salt
4 cups milk
¼ cup butter
2 eggs
½ cup sugar
1 tsp. vanilla
½ cup raisins
nutmeg

Bring water, rice and salt to a boil and cook 7 minutes. Add milk and butter; bring to a boil. Reduce heat, cover and simmer for 1 to 1¼ hours. Beat eggs, sugar and vanilla and add to rice mixture. Remove from heat and add raisins.

Turn into 13x9 pan and sprinkle with nutmeg. Cover with plastic wrap and chill. May also be served warm.

Kiss Pudding

Ethel Kvalheim of Stoughton, Wis., sent this recipe. A well-known rosemaler, she was one of the earliest winners of the Medal of Honor for work in rosemaling.

4 eggs, separated
¼ cup sugar
dash salt
2 cups milk, scalded
1 tsp. vanilla
2/3 cup powdered sugar
2 squares chocolate, melted

Beat egg yolks slightly. Add sugar, salt and slightly cooled milk. Cook in double boiler, stirring constantly until mixture coats spoon. Add vanilla. Spoon into serving dishes.

Beat egg whites until stiff. Fold in powdered sugar and melted chocolate. Put on top of custard. Chill and serve. Serves 4.

The decoration on butter molds was made by carving designs in reverse to stand out in relief on the molded butter.

In this 1801 mold, the Lion of Norway and the crest of the King of Denmark are at right. Vesterheim collection.

Lemon Fromage with Raspberry Sauce
Citronfromasj med bringebœrsaus

Estelle Knudsen of Eden Prairie, Minn., staff member of the Norwegian-American Museum in Decorah, Iowa, sent this recipe. She founded the Nordic Brunch and Nordic Dinner. Estelle writes: "The dinner was designed for the overflow from the sold-out brunch. It is a joint venture of Norwegian-American Museum members from St. Paul and Minneapolis. This recipe, used for the 1980 Nordic Dinner, came from Norway."

1 3-oz. pkg. lemon-flavored gelatin
1 cup hot water
1 cup orange juice, strained
1 cup heavy cream, whipped
1½ tsp. grated lemon rind
Sauce:
1 10-oz. pkg. frozen raspberries
¾ cup red currant jelly
1 Tbsp. cornstarch
sugar

Dissolve gelatin in hot water. Add orange juice and refrigerate until the consistency of egg whites. Remove from refrigerator and beat until frothy. Fold in whipped cream and lemon rind. Pour into chilled and lightly oiled mold. Chill. When firm, unmold. Serve with fresh raspberries and raspberry sauce.

To make sauce, press thawed raspberries through food mill. Heat together ¾ cup of this purée with the currant jelly. Blend cornstarch into remaining ¼ cup of the purée. Add to jelly mixture and cook until thick and clear. Sprinkle with granulated sugar to prevent a layer from forming on top. Cool. Makes 8 servings.

Black and White Fluff
Citronfromage med frukt

Gina J. Hanson Hanson, Forest City, Iowa, the mother of John K. Hanson and Barbara Hanson Bulman.
"A family favorite all through the years when the children were at home. It's easily and quickly put together and can be made ahead and ready to serve for any special meal. Serving in your footed crystal makes it attractive."

1½ cups prunes
2 bananas
12 marshmallows
2 cups whipping cream
½ tsp. lemon extract
maraschino cherries

Wash prunes and boil in enough water to cover until tender, about 10 minutes. Drain and chill. Remove pits, and cut prunes into small pieces. Slice bananas, dip in lemon juice to prevent discoloring. Cut marshmallows in 8 pieces each.

Whip cream. Add lemon extract, prunes, bananas and marshmallows. Mix lightly. Serve in footed glass dishes. Top each serving with a maraschino cherry.

Variation: You can use miniature marshmallows and whipped topping to simplify the preparation of this dessert.

"Veiled Peasant Girls"
Tilslørtebondepiker

Sigurd Daasvand was editor of the Norwegian newspaper Nordisk Tidende *in Brooklyn, N.Y., for 11 years before retiring in 1982 to Oslo, Norway.*

**2 cups dark bread crumbs or
   graham cracker crumbs
2 Tbsp. butter
   applesauce or raspberry jam
   whipped cream**

Grate stale, dark bread or graham cracker crumbs and brown in frying pan in butter. If bread crumbs are used, add a tablespoon of sugar.

When mixture is cool, place in a pudding dish in layers alternately with flavored applesauce or raspberry jam. Let stand in refrigerator overnight, or for a few hours, and serve with whipped cream.

Curds and Whey
Dravle

Norma Anderson Wangsness of Decorah, Iowa. "This is a recipe made by my mother Christine Lotvedt Anderson. It was my favorite. The way Mother turned the cheese chunks with such tender care was truly an art form. My big brother liked the curds and I loved the whey so there were no family feuds over dravle."

**2 quarts sweet milk
2 eggs
1 quart buttermilk
1½ cups sugar
1 cup raisins
3 Tbsp. cornstarch
3 Tbsp. cream or milk**

Cook sweet milk until it comes to a boil. Beat eggs into buttermilk and add to hot milk slowly. When cheese settles, turn down heat for 15 to 20 minutes and simmer. Then turn heat up and cook ½ hour or more. Add the sugar and raisins. Thicken with the cornstarch mixed with cream or milk. When finished, you have curds and whey.

When cooking, handle very gently so as not to break the cheese curds. A wooden spoon is good to stir with. You may turn cheese chunks *gently* several times while cooking.

Sour Milk and Flatbread
Hedmark flatbrødsoll

Rolf H. Erickson of Evanston, Ill., is on the board of directors of Vesterheim and the Norwegian-American Historical Association. He documents histories of immigrants by collecting their artifacts and archival material. He is currently gathering information on Norwegian-American landmarks, painters, sculptors and composers.

"When cousin Jenny Knutsen served us dinner at her apartment in Hamar, Norway, the summer of 1979 she served a dessert called flatbrødsoll. *She cautioned, 'You might not like this, but it is a dish great-grandfather Knut Ramseth would surely have known. It's an old Hedmark specialty.' It was soured milk spooned over crumbled flatbread. I liked it very much and have made something like it."*

**1 16-oz. carton low-calorie plain
   yogurt
2 cups low-fat dry cottage cheese
2 percent lowfat milk
   Ideal flatbread
   sugar, optional**

Mix yogurt, cottage cheese and enough milk to make mixture the consistency of a sauce. "I bring it to the table cold in a sauce dish and let my guests serve themselves by spooning it over crumbled Ideal flatbread. Sugar may be sprinkled over the top. This makes a refreshing first course with *smorbrød*, ideal for summer and ideal for those of us who watch calories."

Nordic Crêpes
Norsk pannekaker

Janice Loomis of Rockford, Mich., is a folk art teacher and an award winner in rosemaling and folk art.

1¼ cups flour
2 Tbsp. sugar
pinch salt
3 eggs
1½ cups milk
2 Tbsp. butter, melted
½ tsp. lemon, rum or brandy extract
Filling:

butter
strawberry jam
powdered sugar
fresh strawberries

Place all ingredients in blender or mixer and beat well. Let batter stand for 1 hour for more perfect crêpes. Use crêpe pan according to directions.

Spread each crêpe with softened butter and strawberry jam. Roll and sprinkle with powdered sugar. Serve with fresh or frozen strawberries.

Norwegian Waffles
Hjemlengsel

Josefa Hansen Andersen of Chicago tells us these waffles are served at many Norwegian Seamen's churches throughout the world. The Norwegian name for the waffles means "longing for home." Mrs. Andersen is treasurer of the Viking Ship Restoration Committee. Her husband Harry is a member of the board of directors of Vesterheim, the Norwegian-American Museum in Decorah, Iowa.

2 eggs
¼ cup sugar
1½ cups flour
1½ tsp. baking powder
1 tsp. baking soda
½ tsp. salt
¼ tsp. ground cardamom
2 cups buttermilk
2 Tbsp. melted butter

Beat eggs and sugar until light and creamy. Mix all dry ingredients and add them to the sugar mixture alternately with the buttermilk. Add melted butter. Brown waffles in waffle iron. These waffles are soft in texture. Serve cold with butter, lingonberries or fruit preserves. They are also served with *gjetost* (goat cheese). Makes 8 to 10 waffles.

Norwegian Pancakes
Pannekaker

Ruth Christoffer Carlsen of Iowa City is the author of eight books for young people, published by Houghton-Mifflin Publishing Company. She writes: "This recipe we use all the time. The pancakes are much like crêpes, but we use them for breakfast with cinnamon and sugar and then roll them. In Norway we found they filled them with lingonberries or strawberries plus whipped cream and we are enthusiastic about that filling."

3 eggs
1 cup flour
1½ cups milk
⅛ tsp. salt
dash cinnamon

Beat eggs slightly with fork. Stir in flour. Add milk and other ingredients and stir until smooth. Batter should be thin. Use a 7-inch skillet with sloped sides. Heat skillet. Pour in small amount of oil. Dip ¼ cup batter, pour in hot pan and quickly tip pan to spread batter over bottom. Slip spatula under cake when top side looks dry. Flip over and brown on other side. Takes only a few seconds. Fold in half or roll on plate.

"To fill, open pancake flat on plate and place a line of butter straight across its center. Cover butter with jam or a sprinkling of sugar and cinnamon (my favorite filling as a child).

"Today we prefer sour cream over raspberries, strawberries or lingonberries with a dusting of powdered sugar. Roll pancake to eat."

Nutty Pumpkin Pie

Vi Thode of Stoughton, Wis., is a nationally noted rosemaler who won the gold medal from the National Rosemaling Exhibit at the Norwegian-American Museum in 1970. She has written four books on rosemaling and has taught rosemaling 20 years.

Although pumpkin pie is uniquely American and certainly not an original Norwegian recipe, it is a favorite to serve Norwegians visiting in American homes. In Decorah, one family serves pie to visiting rosemaling teachers because pie is a dessert unfamiliar to Norwegians.

Marion Nelson, director of Vesterheim, said that in Norway pumpkins are fed to the animals so Norwegians visiting America who are served pumpkin pie "approach it very cautiously and end up loving it."

    1 16-oz. can pumpkin
    5 eggs
    1½ cups sugar
    1 tsp. salt
    2 heaping Tbsp. flour
    2 tsp. cinnamon
    2 tsp. nutmeg
    2 tsp. mace
    1 tsp. allspice
    1 tsp. ginger
    ½ tsp. cloves
    2 tsp. vanilla
    3½ cups milk
    2 uncooked pie crusts
    ½ cup finely chopped walnuts,
        hickory nuts or pecans
        prepared whipped topping or
        whipped cream

Put pumpkin in electric mixer bowl, add eggs and mix well. In a two-cup measuring cup, put sugar, salt, flour and spices. Mix and add to mixer bowl. Let mix. Add vanilla and milk and mix until well blended. Pour into two uncooked pie crusts. Sprinkle half of nuts on each pie. Set pies on one large cookie sheet or two small ones. Bake 1 hour at 375 degrees F. or until done.

This pie freezes well. Serve with dollops of whipped cream. Two pies will serve 10 people.

Grandmother's Buttermilk Doughnuts

Agnes Kjome of Decorah, who is a volunteer at Vesterheim.

    1 egg, well-beaten
    1½ cups fresh thick buttermilk
    4 cups flour
    1 tsp. soda
    1 tsp. salt
    ½ tsp. cinnamon
    ¼ tsp. nutmeg
    1 cup sugar
    4 Tbsp. melted vegetable shortening
    1 tsp. vanilla, optional
        oil for frying

Mix beaten egg and milk. Put flour, soda, salt, spices and sugar in large bowl. Add egg and milk mixture. Add melted shortening and mix well. Add vanilla, if desired. Turn out on lightly floured board. Roll dough out to 1/3-inch thickness. Cut and fry in hot oil at 425 degrees F., turning when doughnuts rise to top. Doughnuts should be a golden brown on both sides and puffed out. Keep oil at same temperature throughout frying. Don't try to fry too many doughnuts at one time. Allow space for floating.

Remove carefully to a paper-covered cookie sheet to drain. Doughnuts may be dipped or rolled in sugar, powdered sugar or icing. Makes 2 to 2½ dozen doughnuts 2½ inches in diameter. Can be frozen or kept in cool place to retain freshness.

Skoal

The term *skoal* (*skål* in Norwegian) is used throughout Scandinavia as a friendly toast. A tale that the word originated when the fierce Vikings drank toasts from the skulls of their dead enemies is at best dubious.

A butter tub of stave construction with double horse-head handle and burnt decoration is in the Vesterheim collection. Giving handles the shape of horse heads is common in Norwegian folk art.

Heritage-Hjemkomst Center

The Heritage-Hjemkomst Interpretive Center of Moorhead, Minnesota, houses a Twentieth Century Viking ship and exhibits that tell the story of the Red River Valley, the trials and dreams of the early settlers, and the important heritage of today's children and adults.

The Hjemkomst (homecoming) Viking Ship was built of lumber from 100 great white oaks. It sailed more than 6,100 miles in 1980 from Duluth, Minnesota to Norway, and triggered the building of the beautiful Center that is attracting visitors from many states.

Exhibits of the Red River Valley Heritage Interpretive Center concern the land, early man, fur trading, settlement, development, farming, "today" and "the future."

"Dare to Dream" is the theme. It fits the building of the Viking ship and the Center, and passes on its challenge to its visitors.